Prophet Muhammad, Stanley aLane-Poole

The Speeches and Table-Talk of the Prophet Mohammad

Prophet Muhammad, Stanley aLane-Poole

The Speeches and Table-Talk of the Prophet Mohammad

ISBN/EAN: 9783337036072

Printed in Europe, USA, Canada, Australia, Japan

Cover: Foto ©Lupo / pixelio.de

More available books at **www.hansebooks.com**

THE
SPEECHES & TABLE-TALK

OF THE

PROPHET MOHAMMAD

Chosen and Translated, with Introduction and Notes,

BY

STANLEY LANE-POOLE

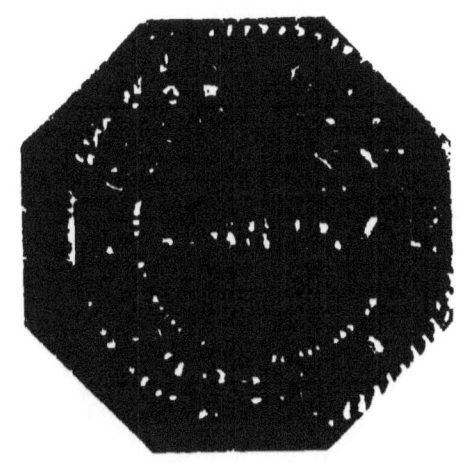

London
MACMILLAN AND CO.
1882

GOD! THERE IS NO GOD BUT HE, THE LIVING, THE STEADFAST! SLUMBER SEIZETH HIM NOT, NOR SLEEP. WHATSOEVER IS IN THE HEAVENS, AND WHATSOEVER IS IN THE EARTH, IS HIS. WHO IS THERE THAT SHALL PLEAD WITH HIM SAVE BY HIS LEAVE? HE KNOWETH WHAT WAS BEFORE THEM AND WHAT SHALL COME AFTER THEM, AND THEY COMPASS NOT AUGHT OF HIS KNOWLEDGE, BUT WHAT HE WILLETH. HIS THRONE OVERSPREADETH THE HEAVENS AND THE EARTH, AND THE KEEPING OF BOTH IS NO BURDEN TO HIM: AND HE IS THE HIGH, THE GREAT!

THE THRONE VERSE, ii. 256.

INTRODUCTION.

THE aim of this little volume is to present all that is most enduring and memorable in the public orations and private sayings of the prophet Mohammad in such a form that the general reader may be tempted to learn a little of what a great man was and of what made him great. At present, it must be allowed that although "Auld Mahound" is a household word, he is very little more than a word. Things are constantly being said, written, and preached about the Arab prophet and the religion he taught, of which an elementary acquaintance with him would show the absurdity. No one would dare to treat the ordinary classics of European literature in this fashion; or, if he did, his exposure would immediately ensue. What I wish to do is to enable any one, at the cost of the least possible exertion, to put himself into a position to judge of popular fallacies about

Mohammad and his creed as surely and certainly as he can judge of errors in ordinary education and scholarship. I do not wish to mention the Korān by name more than can be helped, for I have observed that the word has a deterrent effect upon readers who like their literary food light and easy of digestion. It cannot, however, be disguised that a great deal of this book consists of the Korān, and it may therefore be as well to explain away as far as possible the prejudice which the ill-fated name is apt to excite. It is not easy to say for how much of this prejudice the standard English translator is responsible. The patient and meritorious George Sale put the Korān into tangled English and heavy quarto,—people read quartos then and did not call them *éditions de luxe*,— his version then appeared in a clumsy octavo, with most undesirable type and paper; finally it has come out in a cheap edition, of which it need only be said that utility rather than taste has been consulted. One can hardly blame any one for refusing to look even at the outsides of these volumes. And the inside,—not the mere outward inside, if I may so say, the type and paper,— but the heart of hearts, the matter itself, is by no means calculated to tempt a reluctant reader. The Korān is there arranged according to the orthodox form, instead of in chronological order,—it must be allowed that the chronological order was not discovered in Sale's time,—and the result is that impression of chaotic indefiniteness which impressed Carlyle so strongly, and which Carlyle has impressed upon most of the present generation. A large disorderly collection of prophetic rhapsody did not prove inviting, as the state of popular knowledge about Mohammad very clearly shows.

The attitude of the multitude towards Sale's Korān was on the whole reasonable. But if the faults that were found there are shown to belong to Sale and not to the Korān, or only partly to it, the attitude should change. In the first place, the Korān is not a large book, and in the second, it is by no means so disorderly and anarchic as is commonly supposed. Reckoned by the number of verses, the Korān is only two-thirds of the length of the New Testament, or, if the wearisome stories of the Jewish patriarchs which Mohammad told and retold are omitted, it is no more than the Gospels and Acts. It has been remarked that the Sunday edition of the *New York Herald* is three times as long. But the real permanent contents of the Korān may be taken at far less even than this estimate. The book is full—I will not say of vain repetitions, for in teaching and preaching repetition is necessary—but of reiterations of certain cardinal articles of faith, and certain standard demonstrations of these articles by the analogy of nature. Like the numerous stories borrowed by Mohammad from the Talmud, which have little but an antiquarian interest, many of these reiterated arguments and illustrations may with advantage be passed over. There is also a considerable portion of the Korān which is devoted to the exposure and confutation of those who, from political, commercial, or religious motives, made it their business to thwart Mohammad in his efforts to reform his people. These personal, one might say party, speeches are valuable only to the biographer and historian of the times. They throw but little light on the character of the man Mohammad himself. They show him, indeed, to be—what we knew him before—a sensitive, irritable man, keenly alive to ridicule and scorn. But for this purpose one instance is sufficient. We do not form our estimate of a great statesman from his moments of irritation, but from those larger utterances which reveal the results of a life's study of men and government. So with Mohammad, we may abandon the personal and temporary element in the Korān, and base our judgment upon those utterances which stand for all time, and deal not with individuals or classes, but with man as he is, in Arabia or England, or where we will. This position is not taken with the object of saving Mohammad from himself. His attacks upon his opponents will bear comparison with those of other statesmen. They are doubtless couched in more barbaric language than we are accustomed to, and where we insinuate, Mohammad curses outright. But in the face of a treacherous and malignant opposition, the Arabian prophet comported himself with singular self-restraint. He only threatened hell-fire, and people of all denominations are still threatened with that every Sunday, to say nothing of Lent. Leaving out the Jewish stories, needless repetitions, and temporary exhortations or personal vindications, the speeches of Mohammad may be set forth in very moderate compass. One speech—*sura,* or chapter, as it is generally called—follows another so much to the same effect, that a limited number will be found to contain all the ideas which a minute study of the whole Korān could collect. I believe there is nothing important, either in doctrine or style, which is not contained in the twenty-eight speeches which fill the first hundred and thirty pages of this small volume. If I were a Mohammadan, I think I could accept the present

INTRODUCTION.

collection as a sufficient representation of what the Korān teaches.

The obscurity of the Korān is largely due to its ordinary arrangement. This consists merely in putting the longest chapters first and the shortest last. The Mohammadans appear to be contented with this curious order, which after all is not more remarkable than that of some other sacred books. German criticism, however, has discovered the method of arranging the Korān in approximately chronological sequence. To explain how this is established would carry me too far, but the results are certain. We can state positively that the chapters of the Korān—or, as I prefer to call them, the speeches of Mohammad—fall into certain definite chronological groups, and if we cannot arrange each individual speech in its precise place, we can at least tell to which group, extending over but few years, it belongs. The effect of this critical arrangement is to throw a perfectly clear light on the development of Mohammad's teaching, and the changes in his style and method. When the Korān is thus arranged—as it is in Mr. Rodwell's charming version, which deserves to be better read than it is—the impression of anarchy disappears, and we see only the growth of a remarkable mind, the alternations of weakness and strength in a gifted soul, the inevitable inconsistencies of a great man. I do not believe any one who reads the speeches of Mohammad as I have arranged them in Professor Nöldeke's chronological order will say that they have no definite aim or coherence. They may be monotonous, and often they are rambling, but their intention and sequence of thought are to me clear as noonday.

It is something more, however, than any supposed length or obscurity that has hitherto scared people from the Korān. The truth is that the atmosphere of our Arabian prophet's thoughts is so different from what we breathe ourselves, that it needs a certain effort to transplant ourselves into it. That it can be done, and done triumphantly, may be proved by Mr. Browning's *Saul*, as Semitic a poem as ever came from the desert itself. We see the whole life and character of the Bedawy in these lines :—

> Oh, our manhood's prime vigour ! No spirit feels waste,
> Not a muscle is stopped in its playing nor sinew unbraced.
> Oh, the wild joys of living ! the leaping from rock unto rock,
> The strong rending of boughs from the fir-tree, the cool silver shock
> Of the plunge in the pool's living water, the hunt of the bear,
> And the sultriness showing the lion is couched in his lair.
> And the meal, the rich dates yellowed over with gold dust divine,
> And the locust flesh steeped in the pitcher, the deep draught of wine,

> And the sleep in the dried river-channel, where bulrushes tell
> That the water was wont to go warbling so softly and well.
> How good is man's life, the mere living! how fit to employ
> All the heart and the soul and the senses for ever in joy.

It is not easy to catch the Arab spirit as Mr. Browning has caught it. Arab poetry is a sealed book to most, even among special Orientalists; they construe it, but it does not move them. The cause is to be found in the abrupt transition of thought which is required if we would enter into the spirit of desert song. The Arab stands in direct contrast to ourselves of the north. He is not in the least like an Englishman. His mind travels by entirely different routes from ours, and his body is built up of much more inflammable materials. His free desert air makes him impatient of control in a degree which we can scarcely understand in an organised community. It is difficult now to conceive a nation without cabinets and secretaries of State and policemen, yet to the Arab these things were not only unknown but inconceivable. He lived the free aimless satisfied life of a child. He was supremely content with the exquisite sense of simple existence, and was happy because he lived. Throughout a life that was full of energy, of passion, of strong endeavour after his ideal of desert perfectness, there was yet a restful sense of satisfied enjoyment, a feeling that life was of a surety well worth living. What his ideal was, and how different from any of the ideals of to-day, we know from his own poetry. It was not in the gentler virtues that he prided himself:—

Had I been a son of Māzin, there had not plundered my herds
    the sons of the child of the dust, Dhuhl, son of Sheybān.
There had straightway arisen to help me a heavy-handed kin,
    good smiters when help is needed, though the feeble bend to the blow:
Men who, when Evil bares before them his hindmost teeth,
    fly gaily to meet him in companies or alone.
They ask not their brother, when he lays before them his wrong
    in his trouble, to give them proof of the truth of what he says.
But as for my people, though their number be not small,
    they are good for naught against evil, however light it be;
They requite with forgiveness the wrong of those that do them wrong,
    and the evil deeds of the evil they meet with kindness and love!
As though thy Lord had created among the sons of men
    themselves alone to fear him, and never one man more.
Would that I had in their stead a folk who, when they ride forth,
    strike swiftly and hard, on horse or on camel borne!

The ideal warrior, however, is not always so fierce as this, as may be seen in the following lament for a departed hero, where a gentler touch mingles in its warlike manliness:—

But know ye if Abdallah be gone, and his place a void?
    no weakling, unsure of hand, and no holder-back was he!
Alert, keen, his loins well girt, his leg to the middle bare,
    unblemished and clean of limb, a climber to all things high:
No wailer before ill-luck, one mindful in all he did,
    to think how his work to-day would live in to-morrow's tale.
Content to bear hunger's pain, though meat lay beneath his hand,
    to labour in ragged shirt that those whom he served might rest.

> If Dearth laid her hand on him, and Famine devoured his store,
>   he gave but the gladlier what little to him they spared.
> He dealt as a youth with Youth, until, when his head grew hoar,
>   and age gathered o'er his brow, to Lightness he said—Begone!

The fierceness of the Arab warrior was tempered by those virtues in which more civilised nations are found wanting. If he was swift to strike, the Arab was also prompt to succour, ready to give shelter and protection even to his worst enemy. The hospitality of the Arab is a proverb, but unlike many proverbs it is strictly true. The last milch-camel must be killed rather than the duties of the host neglected. The chief of a clan —not necessarily the richest man in it, but the strongest and wisest—set the example in all Arab virtues, and his tent was so placed in the camp that it was the first the enemy would attack, and also the first that the wayworn traveller would approach. Beacons were lighted hard by to guide wanderers to the hospitable haven, and any man, of whatever condition, who came to the Arab nobleman's tent and said, "I throw myself on your honour," was safe from pursuit even at the cost of his host's life. Honour, like hospitality, meant more than it does now; and the Arab chieftain's pledge of welcome meant protection, unswerving fidelity, help, and succour. Like his pride of birth, devotion to the clan, courage, and generosity, this hospitable trusty friendship of the Arab belongs no doubt to the barbarous virtues of the old world; but it is just these parts of barbarism which civilisation might profitably emulate.

As a friend and as an enemy there was no ambiguity about the Arab. In both relations he was frank, generous, and fearless. And the same may be said of his love. The Arab of the Days of Ignorance, as Mohammadans style the time before the birth of their prophet, was the forerunner of the best side of mediæval chivalry, which indeed is forced to own an Arabian origin. The Arab chief was as much a knight-errant in love as he was a chivalrous opponent in fight. The position of the women of Arabia before the coming of Mohammad has often been commiserated. That women were probably held in low esteem in the town-life which formed an important factor in the Arabian polity is probably true; savage virtues are apt to disappear in the civilised society of cities. But poetry is a good test of a nation's character, —not, perhaps, of a highly civilised nation, for then affectation and the *vogue* come into play,—but undoubtedly of a partly savage nation, where poets only say what they and their fellow men feel. Arabian poetry is full of a chivalrous reverence for women. Allowing for difference of language and the varieties of human nature, it is much more reverent than a great deal of the poetry of our own country to-day. In the old days, says an ancient writer, the true Arab had but one love, and her he loved till death. The Bedawy or Arab of the desert, though he was not above a certain amount of gallantry of a romantic and exciting order, regarded women as divinities to be worshipped, not as chattels to possess. The poems are full of instances of the courtly respect, "full of state and ancientry," displayed by the heroes of the desert towards defenceless maidens, and the mere existence of so general an ideal of conduct in the poems is a strong argument for Arab chivalry; for with the Arabs the abyss between the ideal accepted of the mind and the attaining thereof in action was narrower than it is among more advanced nations. We remember the story of Antar, the Bayard of pagan Arabia, who gave his life to guard some helpless women; and recall these verses of Muweylik, which breathe a tender chivalrous regret for an only love :—

> Take thou thy way by the grave wherein thy dear one lies—
>   Umm el-'Alā—and lift up thy voice : ah ! if she could hear !
> How art thou come, for very fearful wast thou, to dwell
>   in a land where not the most valiant goes but with quaking heart?
> God's love be thine and His mercy, O thou dear lost one !
>   not meet for thee is the place of shadow and loneliness.

INTRODUCTION. xvii

> And a little one hast thou left behind—God's ruth on her!
>   she knows not what to bewail thee means, yet weeps for thee,
> For she misses those sweet ways of thine which thou hadst with her,
>   and the long night wails, and we strive to hush her to sleep in vain.
> When her crying smites in the night upon my sleepless ears,
>   straightway mine eyes brimful are filled from the well of tears.

If anywhere poetry is a gauge of national character, it was so in Arabia, for nowhere was it more a part of the national life. That line, "to think how his work to-day would live in to-morrow's tale," is a true touch. The Arabs were before all things a poetical people. It is not easy to judge of this poetry in translation, even in the fine renderings which I have taken above from Mr. C. J. Lyall, but its effect on the Arabs themselves was unmistakeable. Damiri has a saying, "Wisdom hath alighted on three things, the brain of the Franks, the hands of the Chinese, and the tongue of the Arabs," and the last is not the least true. They had an annual fair, the *Académie française* of Arabia, where the poets of rival clans recited their masterpieces before immense audiences, and received the summary criticism of the multitude. This fair of Okadh was a literary congress, without formal judges, but with unbounded influence. It was here that the polished heroes of the desert determined points of grammar and prosody ; here the seven " Golden Songs " were sung, although (alas for the legend!) they were *not* afterwards suspended in the Kaaba; and here "a magical language, the language of the Hijaz," was built out of the dialects of Arabia and made ready to the skilful hand of Mohammad, that he might conquer the world with his Korān.

Hitherto we have been looking at but one side of Arab life. The Bedawis were indeed the bulk of the race and furnished the swords of the Muslim conquests; but there was also a vigorous town-life in Arabia, and the citizens waxed rich with the gains of their trafficking. For through Arabia ran the trade-route between east and west: it was the Arab traders who carried the produce of the Yemen to the markets of Syria; and how ancient was their commerce one may divine from the words of a poet of Judaea, spoken more than a thousand years before the coming of Mohammad—

> Wedan and Javan from San'a paid for thy produce:
> > sword-blades, cassia, and calamus were in thy trafficking.
>
> Dedan was thy merchant in saddle-cloths for riding.
> Arabia and all the merchants of Kedar, they were the merchants of thy hand;
> > in lambs and rams and goats, in these were they thy merchants.
>
> The merchants of Sheba and Raamah, they were thy merchants;
> > with the chief of all spices, and with every precious stone, and gold, they paid for thy produce.
>
> EZEKIEL xxvii. 19-22.

Mekka was the centre of this trading life, the

typical Arab city of old times, a stirring little town, with its caravans bringing the silks and woven stuffs of Syria and the far-famed damask, and carrying away the sweet-smelling produce of Arabia, frankincense, cinnamon, sandal-wood, aloe and myrrh, and the dates and leather and metals of the south, and the goods that came to the Yemen from Africa and even India; its assemblies of merchant-princes in the Council Hall near the Kaaba; and again its young poets running over with love and gallantry; its Greek and Persian slave-girls brightening the luxurious banquet with their native songs, when as yet there was no Arab school of music and the monotonous but not unmelodious chant of the camel-driver was the national song of Arabia; and its club, where busy men spent their idle hours in playing chess and draughts, or in gossiping with their acquaintance. It was a little republic of commerce, too much infected with the luxuries and refinements of the states it traded with, yet retaining enough of the free Arab nature to redeem it from the charge of effeminacy. Mekka was a home of music and poetry, and this characteristic lasted into Muslim times. There is a story of a certain stonemason who had a wonderful gift of singing. When he was at work the young men used to come and importune him, and bring him gifts of money and food to induce him to sing. He would then make a stipulation that they should first help him with his work. And forthwith they would strip off their cloaks, and the stones would gather round him rapidly. Then he would mount a rock and sing, whilst the whole hill was coloured red and yellow with the variegated garments of his audience. It was, however, in this town-life that the worst qualities of the Arab came out; it was here that his raging passion for dicing and his thirst for wine were most prominent. In the desert there was no great opportunity for indulging in either luxury, but in a town which often welcomed a caravan bringing goods to the value of twenty thousand pound such excesses were to be looked for. Excited by the songs of the Greek slave-girls, and the fumes of mellow wine, the Mekkan would throw the dice till, like the German of Tacitus, he had staked and lost his own liberty.

But Mekka was more than a centre of trade and of song. It was the focus of the religion of the Arabs. Thither the tribes went up every year to kiss the black stone which had fallen from heaven in the primeval days of Adam, and to make the seven circuits of the Kaaba, naked,—for they would not approach God in the garments in which

INTRODUCTION.   xxi

they had done their sins,—and to perform the other ceremonies of the pilgrimage. The Kaaba, a cubical building in the centre of Mekka, was the most sacred temple in all Arabia, and it gave its sanctity to all the district around. It was built, saith tradition, by Adam from a heavenly model, and then rebuilt from time to time by Seth and Abraham and Ishmael, and less reverend persons, and it contained the sacred things of the land. Here was the black stone, here the great god of red agate, and the three hundred and sixty idols, one for each day of the year, which Mohammad afterwards destroyed in one day. Here was Abraham's stone, and that other which marked the tomb of Ishmael, and hard by was Zemzem, the God-sent spring which gushed from the sand when the forefather of the Arabs was perishing of thirst.

The religion of the ancient Arabs, little as we know of it, is especially interesting inasmuch as the Arabs longest retained the original Semitic character, and hence probably the original Semitic religion; and thus in the ancient cult of Arabia we may see the religion once professed by Chaldeans, Canaanites, Israelites, and Phœnicians. This ancient religion "rises little higher than animistic polydaemonism; it is a collection of tribal religions standing side by side, only loosely united, though there are traces of a once closer connection." The great objects of worship were the sun, and the stars, and the three moon-goddesses,—El-Lāt, the bright moon, Menāh, the dark, and El-'Uzza, the union of the two—whilst a lower cultus of trees, stones, and mountains shows that the religion had not quite risen above simple fetishism. There are traces of a belief in a supreme God behind this pantheon, and the moon-goddesses and other divinities were regarded as daughters of the Most High God (Allāh ta'āla). The various deities (but not the supreme Allāh) had their fanes where human sacrifices, though rare, were not unknown; and their cult was superintended by a hereditary line of seers, who were held in great reverence, but never developed into a priestly caste.

Besides the tribal gods, individual households had their special *penates*, to whom was due the first and the last salām of the returning or outgoing master. But in spite of all this superstitious apparatus the Arabs were never a religious people. In the old days, as now, they were reckless, sceptical, materialistic. They had their gods and their divining arrows, but they were ready to demolish both if the responses proved contrary to their wishes. An Arab, who wished to avenge the death of his father, went to consult the square block of white stone called El-Khalasa, by means of divining arrows. Three times he tried, and each time he drew the arrow forbidding vengeance. Then he broke the arrows, and flung them in the face of the idol, crying, "Wretch! if it had been *your* father who was murdered, you would not have forbidden me to avenge him!" The great majority believed in no future life, nor in a reckoning day of good and evil. If a few tied camels to the graves of the dead that the corpse might ride mounted to the judgment-seat, they must have done so more by force of superstitious habit than anything else.

Christianity and Judaism had made but small impress upon the Arabs. There were Jewish tribes in the north, and there is evidence in the Korān and elsewhere that the traditions and rites of Judaism were widely known in Arabia. But the creed was too narrow and too exclusively national to commend itself to the majority of the people. Christianity fared even worse. Whether or not St. Paul went there, it is at least certain that very little effect was produced by the preaching of Christianity in Arabia. We hear of Christians on the borders, and even two or three among the

Mekkans, and bishops and churches are spoken of at Dhafār and Nejrān. But the Christianity that the Arabs knew was, like the Judaism of the northern tribes, a very imperfect reflection of the faith it professed to be. It had become a thing of the head instead of the heart, and the refinements of monophysite and monothelite doctrines gained no hold on the Arab mind.

Thus Judaism and Christianity, though they were well known, and furnished many of the ideas and most of the ceremonies of Islām, were never able to effect any general settlement in Arabia. The common Arabs did not care much about any religion, and the finer spirits found the wrangling dogmatism of the Christian and the narrow isolation of the Jew little to their mind. For there were men before the time of Mohammad who were dissatisfied with the low fetishism in which their countrymen were plunged, and who protested emphatically against the idle and often cruel superstitions of the Arabs. Not to refer to the prophets, who, as the Korān relates, were sent in old times to the tribes of Ad and Thamūd to convert them, there was, immediately before the preaching of Mohammad, a general feeling that a change was at hand; a prophet was expected, and women were anxiously hoping for male children, if so be they might mother the Apostle of God; and the more thoughtful minds, tinged with traditions of Judaism, were seeking for what they called the "religion of Abraham." These men were called "Hanīfs," or "incliners," and their religion seems to have consisted chiefly in a negative position,—in denying the superstition of the Arabs, and in only asserting the existence of one sole-ruling God whose absolute slaves are all mankind—without being able to decide on any minor doctrines, or to determine in what manner this One God was to be worshipped. So long as the Hanīfs could give their countrymen no more definite creed than this, their influence was limited to a few inquiring and doubting minds. It was reserved for Mohammad to formulate the faith of the Hanīfs in the dogmas of Islām.

It is essential to bear in mind all these surroundings of Mohammad if we would understand his position and influence. A desert Arab in love of liberty and worship of nature's beauty, but lacking something of the frank chivalrous spirit of the desert warrior—more a saint than a knight,—yet possessing a patient determined perseverance which belonged to the life of the town, a moral force which the roaming Bedawy did not need, Mohammad owed something to either side of

Arabian life; whilst without the influence of other religions, especially the Jewish, he could never have come forward as the preacher of Islām. Even the old nature worship of the Arabs had its share in the new religion, and no faith was made up of more varied materials than that which Mohammad impressed upon so large a portion of mankind.

Of his early life very little is known. He was born in A.D. 571, and came of the noble tribe of the Koreysh, who had long been guardians of the sacred Kaaba. He lost both his parents early, and as his branch of the tribe had become poor, his duty was to betake himself to the hillsides and pasture the flocks of his neighbours. In after years he would look back with pleasure on these days, and say that God took never a prophet save from among the sheep-folds. The life on the hills gave him the true shepherd's eye for nature which is seen in every speech of the Korān; and it was in those solitary watches under the silent sky, with none near to distract him, that he began those earnest communings with his soul which made him in the end the prophet of his nation. Beyond this shepherd life and his later and more adventurous trade of camel-driver to the Syrian caravans of his rich cousin, Khadīja, whom he presently married at the age of twenty-five, there is little that can be positively asserted of Mohammad's youth. He must have witnessed the poets' contests at the Fair of 'Okadh, and listened to the earnest talk of the Jews and Hanīfs who visited the markets; he may have heard a little, dimly, of Jesus of Nazareth; what he did we know not; what he was is expressed in the nickname by which he was known—" El-Amīn," the Trusty.

"Mohammad was of the middle height, rather thin, but broad of shoulders, wide of chest, strong of bone and muscle. His head was massive, strongly developed. Dark hair, slightly curled, flowed in a dense mass almost to his shoulders; even in advanced age it was sprinkled with only about twenty gray hairs, produced by the agonies of his 'Revelations.' His face was oval-shaped, slightly tawny of colour. Fine long arched eyebrows were divided by a vein, which throbbed visibly in moments of passion. Great black restless eyes shone out from under long heavy eyelashes. His nose was large, slightly aquiline. His teeth, upon which he bestowed great care, were well set, dazzling white. A full beard framed his manly face. His skin was clear and soft, his complexion 'red and white,' his hands were as 'silk and satin,' even as those of a woman. His step was quick and elastic, yet firm as that of one who steps 'from a high to a low place.' In turning his face he would also turn his whole body. His whole gait and presence were dignified and imposing. His countenance was mild and pensive. His laugh was rarely more than a smile.

"In his habits he was extremely simple, though he bestowed great care on his person. His eating and drinking, his dress and his furniture retained, even when he had reached the fulness of power, their almost primitive nature. The only luxuries he indulged in were, besides arms, which he highly prized, a pair of yellow boots, a present from the Negus of Abyssinia. Perfumes, however, he loved passionately, being most sensitive to smells. Strong drink he abhorred.

"His constitution was extremely delicate. He was nervously afraid of bodily pain; he would sob and roar under it. Eminently unpractical in all common things of life, he was gifted with mighty powers of imagination, elevation of mind, delicacy and refinement of feeling. 'He is more modest than a virgin behind her curtain,' it was said of him. He was most indulgent to his inferiors, and would never allow his awkward little page to be scolded whatever he did. 'Ten years,' said Anas his servant, 'was I about the Prophet, and he never said as much as "uff" to me.' He was very affectionate towards his family. One of his boys died on his breast in the smoky house of the nurse, a blacksmith's wife. He was very fond of children; he would stop them in the streets and pat their little heads. He never struck any one in his life. The worst expression he ever made use of in conversation was, 'What has come to him? may his forehead be darkened with mud!' When asked to curse some one, he replied, 'I have not been sent to curse, but to be a mercy to mankind.' 'He visited the sick, followed any bier he met, accepted the invitation of a slave to dinner, mended his own clothes, milked the goats, and waited upon himself,' relates summarily another tradition. He never first withdrew his hand out of another man's palm, and turned not before the other had turned.

"He was the most faithful protector of those he protected, the sweetest and most agreeable in conversation. Those who saw him were suddenly filled with reverence; those who came near him loved him; they who described him would say, 'I have never seen his like either before or after.' He was of great taciturnity, but when he spoke it was with emphasis and deliberation, and no one could forget what he said. He was, however, very nervous and restless withal; often low-spirited, downcast, as to heart and eyes. Yet he would at times suddenly break through these broodings, become gay, talkative, jocular, chiefly among his own. He would then delight in telling little stories, fairy tales, and the like. He would romp with the children and play with their toys."

"He lived with his wives in a row of humble cottages, separated from one another by palm-branches, cemented together with mud. He would kindle the fire, sweep the floor, and milk the goats himself. The little food he had was always shared with those who dropped in to partake of it. Indeed, outside the prophet's house was a bench or gallery, on which were always to be found a number of poor, who lived entirely upon his generosity, and were hence called 'the people of the bench.' His ordinary food was dates and water, or barley bread; milk and honey were luxuries of which he was fond, but which he rarely allowed himself. The fare of the desert seemed most congenial to him, even when he was sovereign of Arabia."

Mohammad was forty before he began his mission of reform. He may long have doubted and questioned with himself, but at least outwardly he seems to have conformed to the popular religion. At length, as he was keeping the sacred months, the God's Truce of the Arabs, in prayer and fasting on Mount Hirā, "a huge barren rock, torn by cleft and hollow ravine, standing out solitary in the full white glare of the desert sun," he thought he heard a voice say " Cry." " What shall I cry?" he answered. And the voice said :—

> " Cry ! in the name of thy Lord, who created—
> Created man from blood.
> Cry ! for thy Lord is the Bountifullest !
> Who taught the pen,
> Taught man what he did not know."
> *Korān*, ch. xcvi.

At first he thought he was possessed with a devil, and the refuge of suicide was often present to his mind. But yet again he heard the voice—" Thou art the Messenger of God, and I am Gabriel." He went back to Khadīja, worn out in body and mind. " Wrap me, wrap me," he cried. And then the word came to him :—

> " O thou who art wrapped, rise up and warn !
> And thy Lord magnify,
> And thy raiment purify,
> And abomination shun !
> And grant not favours to gain increase !
> And wait for thy Lord !"—*Korān*, ch. lxxiv.

These are the first two revelations that came to Mohammad. That he believed he heard them spoken by an angel from heaven is beyond doubt. His temperament was nervous and excitable from a child up. It is said he was subject to cataleptic fits, like Swedenborg; and at least it is certain that his constitution was more delicately and highly strung than most men's. If it is any satisfaction to the incredulous to find evidence of a special tendency towards hallucinations, the proofs are at hand. But whether the "revelations" were subjective or not makes no difference to the result. Whencesoever they came, they were real and potent revelations to the man and to his people.

After this beginning of converse with the supernatural, or whatever we prefer to term it, the course of Mohammad's revelations—the speeches which make up the Korān—flowed unbroken for twenty years and more. They fall naturally into two great divisions—the period of struggle at Mekka, and the period of triumph at Medina; and the characteristics of the two are diverse as the circumstances which called them forth. For whatever Mohammad himself thought of his revelations, to modern criticism they are speeches or sermons strictly connected with the religious and political circumstances of the speaker's time. In the first period we see a man possessed of a strong religious idea, an idea dominating his life, and his one aim is to impress that idea on his people, the inhabitants of Mekka. He preached to them in season and out of season;

whenever the spirit moved him he poured forth his burning eloquence into the ears of a suspicious and incredulous audience. Three years of unwearied effort produced the pitiful result of a score or so of converts, mainly from the poorest classes. In the fifth year even these were compelled by the persecutions of the Koreysh to take refuge in Abyssinia —"a land of righteousness, wherein no man is wronged." Mohammad had by this time advanced from a mere inculcation of the doctrine of one all-powerful God to a plain attack upon the idolatry of the Mekkans; and the Koreysh, as guardians of the Kaaba and receivers of the pilgrims' tolls, were keenly alive to the consequences which the overthrow of the sacred temple would entail upon its keepers. The result of Mohammad's bold denunciations was a cruel persecution of his humbler followers, and their consequent flight to Abyssinia; he himself was too nearly allied to powerful chiefs to be lightly injured in a land where the blood-revenge held sway. Presently the devotion of the prophet, his manly bearing under obloquy and reproach, and above all, the winged words of his eloquence, brought several men of influence and wealth into his faith, and in the sixth year of his mission Mohammad found himself surrounded no longer by a crowd of slaves and beggars, but by tried swordsmen, chiefs of great families, leaders in the councils of Mekka; and the new sect performed their rites no more in secret, but publicly at the Kaaba, in the face of the whole city. The Koreysh resolved on stronger measures. After trying vainly to isolate him from his family—the true Arab spirit of kindred was not so easily shaken—they put the whole clan under a ban, and swore they would not marry with them, nor buy nor sell with them, nor hold with them any intercourse soever. To the credit of Mohammad and of his clan, only one man of them refused to share his fate, though most of them did not hold with his doctrines. Sooner than give up their kinsman, they went, every man of them, save that one, into their own quarter of the city, and there abode in banishment for two years. Starvation was busy with the incarcerated family, when the Koreysh grew ashamed of their work, and five chiefs arose and put on their armour and went to the ravine where the banished people were shut up, and bade them come forth.

The time of inaction was followed by a time of sorrow. Mohammad lost his wife and the aged chief, his uncle, who had hitherto been his protector. All Mekka was against him, and in despair of heart he journeyed to Taif, seventy miles away, and told his message to another folk: but they stoned him for three miles from the town. The time, however, was coming when a distant city would hold out welcoming hands to the prophet whom Mekka and Taif had rejected. As he dwelt-on disconsolately at Mekka, pilgrims from Yethrib (soon to be known as Medina or Medīnet-en-Neby, "the Prophet's City") hearkened to the new doctrine, and carried it home to their own folk. Jews had prepared the way for Islām at Medina; the new religion did not seem preposterous to those who had long heard of One God; and presently the Faithful began to leave Mekka in small companies, and take refuge in the hospitable city where their prophet was honoured. At length Mohammad, when like the captain of a sinking ship he had seen his followers safely away, accompanied by one faithful friend eluded the vigilance of the Koreysh, and safely arrived at Medina in the early summer of 622. This is the Hijra or "Flight" of Mohammad, from which the Muslims date their history.

During these years of struggle and persecution at Mekka 90 out of the 114 chapters or speeches which compose the Korān were revealed, amounting to about two-thirds of the whole book. All these speeches are inspired with but one great design, and are in strong contrast with the complicated character of the later chapters issued at Medina. In the Mekka chapters Mohammad appears in the unalloyed character of a prophet: he has not yet assumed the functions of a statesman and lawgiver. His object is not to give men a code or a constitution, but to call them to the worship of the One God. There is hardly a word of other doctrines, scarcely anything of ritual, or social or penal regulations. Every speech is directed simply to the grand design of the Prophet's life, to convince men of the unutterable majesty of the One God, who brooks no rivals. Mohammad appeals to the people to credit the evidence of their own eyes; he calls to witness the wonders of nature, the stars in their courses, the sun and the moon, the dawn cleaving asunder the dark veil of night, the life-giving rain, the fruits of the earth, life and death, change and decay—all are " signs of God's power, if only ye would understand." Or he tells the people how it fared with older generations, when prophets came to them and exhorted them to believe in One God and do righteousness, and they rejected them; how there fell upon the unbelieving nation grievous woe. How was it with the people of Noah? he asks :—they were drowned in the flood because they would not hearken to his words. And the people of the Cities of the Plain? And Pharaoh and his host? And the old tribes of the Arabs who would not hear the warnings of their prophets? One answer follows each—there came upon them a great calamity. "These are the true stories," he cries, "and there is only One God! and yet ye turn aside." Eloquent appeals to the signs of nature, threats of a day of reckoning to come, warnings drawn from the legends of the prophets, arguments for the truth and reality of the revelation, make up the substance of this first division of the Korān.

In the earliest group of speeches delivered at Mekka, forty-eight in number, belonging to what is called the First Period, extending over the first four years of Mohammad's mission, we feel the poetry of the man. Mohammad had not lived among the sheep-folds in vain, and spent long solitary nights gazing at the silent heaven and watching the dawn break over the mountains. This earliest portion of the Korān is one long blazonry of nature's beauty. How can you believe in aught but the One omnipotent God when you see this glorious world around you and this wondrous tent of heaven above you? is Mohammad's frequent question to his countrymen. "All things in heaven and earth supplicate Him; then which of the bounties of your Lord will ye deny?" There is little but this appeal to nature in the first part of the speeches at Mekka. The prophet was in too exalted a state during these early years to stoop to argument; he rather seeks to dazzle the sense with brilliant images of God's workings in creation. "Verily in the creation of the heavens and the earth are signs to you, if ye would understand." His sentences have a rhythmical ring though they are not in true metre. The lines are very short, yet with a musical cadence. The meaning is often but half expressed. The poet seems impatiently to stop as if he despaired of explaining himself: he has essayed a thing beyond words, has discovered the impotence of language, and broken off with the sentence unfinished. The style is throughout fiery and impassioned. The words are those of a man whose whole heart is bent on convincing, and they carry with them even now the impression of the burning vehemence with which they were originally hurled forth. These earliest speeches are generally brief. They are pitched too high to be long sustained. We feel we have here to do with a poet as well as a preacher, and that his poetry costs him too much to be spun out.

In urging to repentance and faith, Mohammad's

great weapon is the judgment to come—the day of retribution, when all mankind shall be arraigned before the throne of God ; and those who have done good shall be given the book of the record of their actions in their right hand, and enjoy abiding happiness in gardens, under which the rivers flow ; whilst the wicked shall receive his damning record in his left hand, and be dragged by heel and hair to hell, to broil therein for ever. The day of judgment is a stern reality to Mohammad. It is never out of his thoughts, and he says himself that if men realised what that day was, they would weep much and laugh little. He is never tired of depicting its terrors, and cannot find names enough to describe it. He calls it the Hour, the Mighty Day, the great Calamity, the Inevitable Fact, the Smiting, the Overwhelming, the Hard Day, the Promised Day, the Day of Decision.

The high poetic fervour of the first group of Mekka speeches is to some extent lost in the Second, and still more in the Third period, corresponding to the fifth and sixth years, and from thence to the Hijra, respectively, and each comprising twenty-one speeches. The change is partly one of style, partly of matter. The verses and the speeches themselves become longer and more rambling ; the resonant oaths by all the wonders of nature are exchanged for the mild asseveration, "By the Korān." There is more self-assertion and formality, and the special words of God are as it were italicised by the prefixed verb, "Say." It must be remembered that the speeches of the Korān are all supposed to be the utterances of God *in propriâ personâ,* of whom Mohammad is only the mouthpiece. The apparent vindications and laudations of the prophet himself are explicable from this point of view; and the reader must never forget it when he is perplexed by the "we" (God), and "thou" (Mohammad), and "ye" (the audience), of the Korān. The most important alteration to be observed in the progress of the orations at Mekka is the introduction of numerous stories derived, with considerable corruptions, from the Jewish Haggadah. More than fifteen hundred verses, nearly a quarter of the Korān, are occupied with wearisome repetitions of these legends. They are to be seen methodically arranged in Lane's *Selections from the Korān,* and I need only say that, with the exception of one or two typical examples (like the speech called *The Moon,* p. 41), and a few digressions in speeches (like *The Children of Israel,* p. 57) that were too important to be omitted, these tales are excluded from the present collection. Their only real in-

INTRODUCTION.

terest is Mohammad's use of them as evidence of the continuity of revelation. He believed that all preceding prophets were inspired of God, and that they taught the same faith as himself. From Adam to Jesus they all brought their messages to their people, and were rejected. He makes them exhort their people in precisely similar words to those with which he exhorts the Koreysh. There is nothing new in his own doctrine, he says, it is but the teaching of Abraham, of Moses, of Christ, of all the prophets. But it is the last and best, the seal of prophecy, after which no other will be given before the Great Day. It supersedes or confirms all that goes before.

Quite half of the second group of Mekka speeches consists of these Jewish legends. There are not so many in the third, and none in the first. But if the Third does not contain quite so many of these tedious fables, it is even tamer in style. Mohammad seems to be cataloguing the signs of nature mechanically, and he is constantly recurring to the charge of forgery which was often brought against him, or to the demand for miracles, which he always frankly admitted he could not gratify. I am only a warner, he said; I cannot show you a sign—a miracle—except what ye see every day and night. Signs are with God: He who could make the heavens could easily show you a sign if He pleased; beware, lest one day ye see a sign indeed, and taste in hell that which ye called a lie! That the old eloquence, in spite of repetition and wearing trouble, was not dead, may be seen from the speech called *Thunder* (p. 104), where the nature painting is as fine as anywhere in the Korān.

The first great division of Mohammad's speeches, then, is oratorical rather than dogmatic. He has a great dogma, indeed, and uses every resource to recommend it. But there is little detail in these ninety Mekka speeches. Hardly any definite laws or precepts are to be found in them, and most of these in the speech entitled *The Children of Israel* (p. 57). Certain general rules of prayer are given, hospitality and thrift are commended in a breath, "Let not thy hand be chained to thy neck, nor yet stretch it out right open;" infanticide, inchastity, homicide (save in blood-revenge), the robbing of orphans, a false balance, usury, a broken covenant, and a proud stomach, are denounced; certain foods are prohibited; and the whole duty of man is thus briefly summed up:—"Say: I am only a man like you: I am inspired that your God is but One God. Then let him who hopeth to meet his Lord do righteousness, and join no (idol) in his worship of God."

There is little here of a complicated ritual or a metaphysical theology. Thus far the social and religious laws which we associate with Islām are not found in the Mohammadan Bible. We hear only the voice crying in the wilderness, "Hear ye, people! The Lord your God is one Lord."

Mohammad's position at Medina was totally different from that he occupied at Mekka. Instead of a struggling reformer, despised and ridiculed by almost every man he met, he was a king, ruling a large city with despotic power, and needing every resource of statecraft to maintain order among its contentious elements. There was a large party, known in the Korān as the "Disaffected" or "Hypocrites," who found it politic to profess Islām, but were ready to avail themselves of any propitious occasion to overturn or injure it. Still more important were the Jewish Arab tribes settled at Medina, who at first hoped to find a tool to their hands in the new prophet, who seemed to teach something very like Judaism; but who, when they found him unmanageable, straightway turned upon him with double malignity, and exerted themselves in all treacherous ways to countermine his authority and help his enemies within and without the city. Mohammad has been blamed for the severity with which he suppressed the rebellious parties in his state, and the sentences of exile and death passed upon the Jews have been regarded as proofs of a vindictive nature. An impartial study of the facts of the case, however, shows plainly that strong measures were needed for the preservation of the Muslim religion and polity; and the vigorous blows struck by Mohammad at rebellion in the beginning probably saved bloodshed afterwards. Whilst the prophet's supremacy was being established and maintained among the mixed population of Medina, a vigorous warfare was carried on outside with his old persecutors, the Koreysh. On the history of this war, consisting as it did mainly of small raids and attacks upon caravans, I need not dwell. Its leading features were the two battles of Bedr and Ohud, in the first of which three hundred Muslims, though outnumbered at the odds of three to one, were completely victorious (A.D. 624, A.H. 2); whilst at Ohud, being outnumbered in the like proportion, and deserted by the "Disaffected" party, they were almost as decisively defeated (A.H. 3). Two years later the Koreysh gathered together their allies, advanced upon Medina, and besieged it for fifteen days; but the foresight of Mohammad in digging a trench, and the enthusiasm of the Muslims in defending it, resisted all assaults, and the coming of the heavy storms for which the climate of Medina is noted drove the enemy back to Mekka. The next year (A.H. 6) a ten years' truce (see *The Victory*, p. 124, and notes) was concluded with the Koreysh, in pursuance of which a strange scene took place in the following spring. It was agreed that Mohammad and his people should perform the Lesser Pilgrimage, and that the Koreysh should for that purpose vacate Mekka for three days. Accordingly in March 629, about two thousand Muslims, with Mohammad at their head on his famous camel, El-Kaswa,—the camel on which he had fled from Mekka,—trooped down the valley and performed the rites which every Muslim to this day observes.

" It was surely a strange sight which at this time presented itself in the vale of Mekka, a sight unique in the history of the world. The ancient city is for three days evacuated by all its inhabitants, high and low, every house deserted; and as they retire, the exiled converts, many years banished from their birthplace, approach in a great body, accompanied by their allies, revisit the empty homes of their childhood, and within the short allotted space fulfil the rites of pilgrimage. The ousted inhabitants, climbing the heights around, take refuge under tents or other shelter among the hills and glens; and clustering on the overhanging peak of Abu-Kubeys, thence watch the movements of the visitors beneath them, as with the Prophet at their head they make the circuit of the Kaaba and the rapid procession between Es-Safā and Marwah; and anxiously scan every figure if perchance they may recognise among the worshippers some long lost friend or relative. It was a scene rendered possible only by the throes which gave birth to Islām." When the three days were over, Mohammad and his party peaceably returned to Medina, and the Mekkans re-entered their homes. But this pilgrimage, and the self-restraint of the Muslims therein, advanced the cause of Islām among its enemies. Converts increased daily, and some leading men of the Koreysh went over to Mohammad. The clans around were sending-in deputations of homage. But the final keystone was set in the 8th year of the flight (A.D. 630), when a body of Koreysh broke the truce by attacking an ally of the Muslims, and Mohammad forthwith marched upon Mekka with ten thousand men, and the city, despairing of defence, surrendered. The day of Mohammad's greatest triumph over his enemies was also the day of his grandest victory over himself. He freely forgave the Koreysh all the years of sorrow and cruel scorn in which they had afflicted him, and gave an amnesty to the whole population of Mekka. Four criminals whom justice condemned made up Mohammad's proscription list when he entered as a conqueror to the city of his bitterest enemies. The army followed his example, and entered quietly and peaceably; no house was robbed, no women insulted. One thing alone suffered destruction. Going to the Kaaba, Mohammad stood before each of the three hundred and sixty idols, and pointed to it with his staff, saying, "Truth is come, and falsehood is fled away!" and at these words his attendants hewed them down, and all the idols and household gods of Mekka and round about were destroyed.

It was thus that Mohammad entered again his native city. Through all the annals of conquest there is no triumphant entry comparable to this one.

The taking of Mekka was soon followed by the adhesion of all Arabia. Every reader knows the story of the spread of Islām. The tribes of every part of the peninsula sent embassies to do homage to the prophet. Arabia was not enough: Mohammad had written in his bold uncompromising way to the great kings of the East—to the Persian Chosroes and the Greek Emperor; and these little knew how soon his invitation to the faith would be repeated, and how quickly Islām would be knocking at their doors with no faltering hand.

The prophet's career was near its end. In the tenth year of the flight, twenty-three years after he had first felt the spirit move him to preach to his people, he resolved once more to leave his adopted city and go to Mekka to perform a farewell pilgrimage. And when the rites were done in the valley of Minā, the prophet spake unto the multitude— the forty thousand pilgrims—with solemn last words :

Ye people, hearken to my words : for I know not whether after this year I shall ever be amongst you here again.

Your lives and your property are sacred and inviolable amongst one another until the end of time.

The Lord hath ordained to every man the share of his inheritance ; a testament is not lawful to the prejudice of heirs.

The child belongeth to the parent, and the violater of wedlock shall be stoned.

Ye people, ye have rights demandable of your wives, and they have rights demandable of you. Treat your women well.

And your slaves, see that ye feed them with such food as ye eat yourselves, and clothe them with the stuff ye wear. And if they commit a fault which ye are not willing to forgive, then sell them, for they are the servants of the Lord and are not to be tormented.

Ye people ! hearken unto my speech and comprehend it. Know that every Muslim is the brother of every other Muslim. All of you are on the same equality : ye are one brotherhood.

Then looking up to heaven he cried, " O Lord, I have delivered my message and fulfilled my mission." And all the multitude answered, " Yea, verily hast thou !"—" O Lord, I beseech thee, bear

INTRODUCTION. xlix

Thou witness to it!" and, like Moses, he lifted up his hands and blessed the people. Three months more and Mohammad was dead,—A.H. 11, A.D. 632.

And when it was noised abroad that the prophet was dead, Omar, the fiery-hearted, the Simon Peter of Islām, rushed among the people and fiercely told them they lied; it could not be true. And Abu-Bekr came and said, "Ye people! he that hath worshipped Mohammad, let him know that Mohammad is dead; but he that hath worshipped God, that the Lord liveth and doth not die."

The altered circumstances of Mohammad's life at Medina produced a corresponding change in his speeches. They are now not so much exhortations to unbelievers as directions and encouragements to the faithful; and instead of being one complete oration, as most of the early speeches are, they are a collection of isolated "rulings" on various points of conduct. The prophet's house at Medina became a court of appeal for the whole body of Muslims. They came to him with all their difficulties,—domestic, social, political, religious,—and asked for direction. Then Mohammad said in few words what he thought right and just; and these decisions have been treated as laws binding upon the Mohammadan world for all time. It is fortunate that Mohammad was a man of sound common sense, or the law of Islām would be a preposterous medley. As it is, it seems clear that the prophet never wished to lay down a code of law, and, instead of volunteering rules of conduct and ritual, used to wait to have them extorted from him by questioning. "God wishes to make things easy for you," he says, "for man was created weak." He seems to have distrusted himself as a lawgiver, for there is a tradition which relates a speech of his in which he cautions the people against taking his decision on worldly affairs as infallible. When he speaks of the things of God he is to be obeyed; but when he deals with human affairs he is only a man like those about him. He was contented to leave the ordinary Arab customs in force except when they were manifestly unjust. The truth is that, as in the Mekka speeches so in those of Medina, the legal and dogmatic element is curiously small. The greater part of those long chapters uttered in fragments at Medina, and then pieced together haphazard by the prophet's amanuenses, consists of diatribes against the Jews and hypocrites, reflections on the conduct of the allies in battle, encouragement after defeat, exhortations as to the future, besides a great deal of personal matter—regulations of the prophet's harem, vindications of his own or his wives' conduct,—and similar things of a temporary and local interest. Though the style is monotonous and longwinded, like the third Mekka period, there are still flashes of the old eloquence, though perhaps it is less spontaneous than of old, such as we hear in the chapter of *Light*—

God is the light of the heavens and the earth; his light is as a niche in which is a lamp, and the lamp in a glass; the glass is as it were a glittering star: it is lit from a blessed tree, an olive neither of the east nor of the west, the oil thereof would wellnigh shine though no fire touched it—light upon light—God guideth to His light whom He pleaseth.

In the houses God hath suffered to be raised, for His name to be commemorated therein, men magnify Him at morn and eve:

Men whom neither merchandise nor trafficking divert from remembering God and being instant in prayer and giving alms, fearing a day when hearts and eyes shall quiver;

That God may recompense them for the best that they have wrought, and give them increase of His grace; for God maketh provision for whom He pleaseth without count.

But those who disbelieve are like a vapour in a plain: the thirsty thinketh it water, till, when he cometh to it, he findeth nothing; but he findeth God with him; and He will settle his account, for God is quick at reckoning:—

Or like black night on a deep sea, which wave above wave doth cover, and cloud over wave, gloom upon gloom,—when one putteth out his hand he can scarcely see it; for to whom God giveth not light, he hath no light.

Hast thou not seen that what is in the heavens and the earth magnifieth God, and the birds on the wing? each one knoweth its prayer and its praise, and God knoweth what they do:

God's is the empire of the heavens and the earth, and to Him must all things return!

Hast thou not seen that God driveth the clouds, and then joineth them, and then heapeth them up, and thou mayest see the rain coming forth from their midst; and He sendeth down from the heaven mountain-clouds with hail therein, and He maketh it fall on whom He pleaseth, and He turneth it away from whom He pleaseth: the flashing of His lightning well nigh consumeth the eyes!—xxiv. 35-43.

The actual legal residue in the Medina chapters is singularly small. Chapters ii., iv., and v., contain nearly all the law of the Korān; but it must be allowed they are very long chapters, and form nearly a tenth part of it. Their practical import,—the definite ruling of Mohammad on dogmatic, ritual, civil, and criminal matters,—is collected in pp. 133-144, and need not be repeated here. The conclusion, however, is worth pointing clearly. The Korān does not contain, even in outline, the elaborate ritual and complicated law which now passes under the name of Islām. It contains merely those decisions which happened to be called for at Medina. Mohammad himself knew that it did not provide for every emergency, and recommended a principle of analogical deduction to guide his followers when they were in doubt. This analogical deduction has been the ruin of Islām. Commentators and jurists have set their nimble wits to work to extract from the Korān legal decisions which an ordinary mind could never discover there; and the whole structure of modern Mohammadanism has been built upon this foundation of sand. The Korān is not responsible for it.

There is, however, another source of information about Mohammad's teaching and practice which is largely responsible for the present form of the once simple creed of Mekka. Besides the public speeches which were held to be directly inspired by God, and indeed copied from a book supposed to exist in the handwriting of God,—the chapters of the Korān,—there were many sayings of Mohammad which were said in a private unofficial way in his circle of intimate friends, and which were almost as carefully treasured up as the others. These are the Traditions, or as I may call them, the Table-Talk of Mohammad, for they correspond more nearly to what we mean by table-talk than any other form of composition. The Table-Talk of Mohammad deals with the most minute and delicate circumstances of life, and is much more serviceable to the lawyer than the Korān itself. The sayings are very numerous and very detailed; but how far they are genuine it is not easy to determine. The Korān is known beyond any doubt to be at this moment, in all practical respects, identical with the prophet's words as collected immediately after his death. How it was edited and collected may be read elsewhere. The only point to be here insisted on is that its genuineness is above suspicion. Unfortunately, as much cannot be said for the Traditions. They were collected at a late period, subjected to a totally useless and preposterous criticism, and thus reduced from 600,000 to 7275, without becoming in the least more trustworthy in the process. It is almost impossible now to sift them with any certainty. All we can go upon is internal evidence, and a few obvious contradictions in date—as when people relate things which they apparently heard before they were born. Beyond this, criticism is helpless, and all we can do is what I have done here—to collect those which strike the attention and do not seem peculiarly improbable, and accept them provisionally as possibly correct reports of Mohammad's table-talk. There are six standard collections of orthodox traditions, but those on pp. 147-182 are taken from an abridgment, the Mishkāt-el-Masābīh, which Captain A. N. Matthews had the patience to translate and publish at Calcutta in 1809. In the midst of such doubt, they are sufficient for the purpose of illustration, without any pretence of completeness or critical precision.

In conclusion, let us banish from our minds any conception of the Korān as a code of law, or a systematic exposition of a creed. It is neither of these. Let us only think of a simple enthusiast confronted with many and varied difficulties, and trying to meet them as best he could by the inward light that guided him. The guidance was not perfect, we know, and there is much that is blameworthy in Mohammad; but whatever we believe of him, let it be granted that his errors were not the result of premeditated imposition, but were the mistakes of an ignorant, impressible, superstitious, but nevertheless noble and great man.

March 1882.

REFERENCES.

In the *Introduction*, pp. xviii.–xxv. and xliv.–xlviii., appeared before in my Introduction to Lane's *Selections from the Kurān*, 2nd ed. (Trübner's Oriental series, 1879), to which I must refer the reader for further information on Mohammad and Islām, and especially concerning the portions of the Korān dealing with the Jewish legends purposely omitted from the present work. Pp. xxxv.–xxxviii. reproduce a few paragraphs from the *Edinburgh Review*, No. 316, October 1881, p. 371, ff. The Arab poetry quoted in the Introduction is from the admirable versions contributed by Mr. C. J. Lyall to the Journal of the Asiatic Society of Bengal, 1877 and 1881. The description of Mohammad's person and mode of life, pp. xxvii.–xxix., is from E. Deutsch, *Literary Remains*, p. 70, ff; and R. Bosworth Smith, *Mohammed and Mohammedanism*, 2d ed., p. 131; to which, and to the Rev. E. Sell's *Faith of Islām*, in many respects the best treatise on the Mohammadan religion, as it now is, that has appeared in recent years, the reader is referred for much concerning modern and historical Mohammadanism which is beyond the design of the present volume.

In the text, I must acknowledge my general indebtedness to the versions of George Sale and the Rev. J. M. Rodwell for many valuable interpretations; but I wish especially to record my obligations to Prof. E. H. Palmer, in respect of some fine renderings which he has been the first to use in his translation of the Korān for the series of *Sacred Books of the East*, and which I have not hesitated to adopt.

S. L.-P.

ANALYTICAL TABLE OF CONTENTS.

                                                    PAGE
INTRODUCTION   v
>   The Korān is capable of adequate representation in small compass and approximately chronological order. The original audience of Mohammad's speeches: Arabian characteristics in desert-life and town-life, poetry and religion. Mohammad's early life, person and habits, call to preach, and work at Mekka. The three periods of Mekka speeches. Change of position at Medina, and consequent change in oratory. The Medina speeches. Incompleteness of the law of the Korān. The Traditions or Table-talk. References.

THE SPEECHES AT MEKKA . . .   1

>   I.—*THE POETIC PERIOD.* Aet. 40-44, A.D. 609-613   1
>
>   THE NIGHT (xcii.)   3
>> The difference between the good and the wicked in their lives and their future states; warning of hell and promise of heaven.

TABLE OF CONTENTS.

	PAGE
THE COUNTRY (xc.)	5

    The steep road to the life to come is by charity and faith.

THE SMITING (ci.)   7

    The terrors of the Judgment Day and the Bottomless Pit.

THE QUAKING (xcix.)   8

    Signs of the Last Day, when all secrets shall be revealed.

THE RENDING ASUNDER (lxxxii.) . .   9

    Signs of the Last Day; man's unbelief; angels record his actions, by which his fate shall be decided.

THE CHARGERS (c.)   11

    Man's ingratitude towards God will be exposed on the Last Day.

SUPPORT (cvii.)   12

    Uncharitable hypocrites denounced.

THE BACKBITER (civ.)   13

    The covetous slanderer shall be cast into Blasting Hell.

THE SPLENDOUR OF MORNING (xciii.) .   14

    The goodness of God towards Mohammad must be imitated towards others.

THE MOST HIGH (lxxxvii.)   15

    God the Creator is to be magnified. Mohammad is enjoined to admonish the people; the opposite fates of those who hearken and those who turn away; the message is the same as that delivered by Abraham and Moses.

THE WRAPPING (lxxxi.) 17
Signs of the Last Day. Authenticity of the Korān: Mohammad neither mad nor possessed. The Korān a reminder, but man is powerless to follow it except by God's decree.

THE NEWS (lxxviii.) 19
Men dispute about the Last Day: yet it shall come as surely as God created all things. The last trump and the gathering of mankind to judgment. Description of the torments of Hell and the delights of Paradise.

THE FACT (lvi.) 22
Signs of the Last Day. The three kinds of men—prophets, righteous, and wicked—and the future state of each. The power of God shown in creation. The Korān true and sacred. The state after death.

THE MERCIFUL (lv.) 27
A *Benedicite* reciting the works of God, and the Judgment and Paradise and Hell, with a refrain challenging genii and mankind to deny His signs.

	PAGE
THE UNITY (cxii.)	32

A profession of faith in one God.

THE FATIHAH (i.)	33

A prayer for guidance and help: the Muslim *Paternoster*.

II.—*THE RHETORICAL PERIOD.* Aet. 44-46, A.D. 613-615 35

THE KINGDOM (lxvii.)	37

The power of God shown in creation: Hell the reward of those who disbelieve in God's messengers and discredit His signs. None but God knows when the Last Day will be.

THE MOON (liv.)	41

The Judgment approaches, but men will not heed the warning, and call it a lie and magic. Even so did former generations reject their apostles: the people of Noah, Ad, Thamūd, Lot, Pharaoh; and there came upon all of them a grievous punishment. Neither shall the men of Mekka escape. Refrain: the certainty of punishment and the heedlessness of man.

K. (l.)	45

Why is the Resurrection so incredible? Does not God continually create and re-create? Former generations were equally incredulous, but they all found the threat of punishment was true. So shall it be again. The recording angels shall bear witness, and hell shall be filled. Who can escape God, who created all things, and to whom all things must one day return?

Y.S. (xxxvi.) 49

Mohammad a true messenger from God to warn the people, whose ancestors would not be warned. God hardens their hearts so that they cannot believe. Everything is written down in the Book of God. Just so did the people of Antioch reject the apostles of Jesus, and stoned the only convert among themselves; and there came a shout from heaven and exterminated them. Why do not men reflect on such warnings? Signs of the Resurrection are seen in the revival of spring and the growth of plants, and the alternations of night and day, and the changes of the sun and moon, and the ships that sail on the sea. Yet they are not convinced! The Last Day shall come upon them suddenly. Paradise and Hell. The Korān not a poem, but a plain warning of God's might and judgment to come. Their idols need protection instead of giving it. God who first made life can quicken it again: his "Fiat" is instantly carried out.

	PAGE
THE CHILDREN OF ISRAEL (xvii.) . .	57

The dream of the journey to Jerusalem. The two sins of the children of Israel and their punishments. The Korān gives promise of a great reward for righteousness and an aching torment for disbelief. Each man shall be judged by his own deeds, and none shall be punished for another's sin; nor was any folk destroyed without warning. Kindness and respect to parents, and duty to kinsfolk and travellers and the poor; hospitality, yet without waste; faithfulness in engagements, and honesty in trading, enjoined. Idolatry, infanticide, inchastity, homicide (except in a just cause and in fair retaliation), and abusing orphans' trust, and pride, forbidden. The angels are not the daughters of God: He has no partner, and the whole creation worships Him. But God hardens people's hearts so that they turn away from the Korān. The Resurrection is nearer than they think. The faithful must speak pleasantly and not wrangle. Mohammad has no power to compel belief. The false gods themselves dread God's torment. The power of working miracles was not given to Mohammad, because the people of yore always disbelieved in them: so Thamūd with the miraculous camel. The story of the devil's original enmity to Adam; but the devil cannot protect his followers against God, to whom belongs all power on land and sea, and whose is the Judgment. Mohammad nearly tempted to temporize. Prayer at sunset and dawn and night vigils commended. Man's insincerity. The spirit sent from God. The Korān inimitable. The demand for miracles and for angelic messengers repudiated. The fate of those who disbelieve in the resurrection. Moses and Pharaoh: the consequences of unbelief. The Korān divided for convenience. The solace of the faithful. God and the Merciful the same deity.

III.—*THE ARGUMENTATIVE PERIOD.* Aet. 46-53, A.D. 615-622 . . . 73

THE BELIEVER (xl.) 75

The revelation is from God. Former generations rejected their apostles and were punished. The angels praise God. The despair of the damned. The great tryst: the judgment of God is unerring. The generations of yore were greater than those of to-day: yet nothing could save them from God. The history of Moses and Pharaoh and the Egyptian convert, and the evil fate of the infidels. The proud shall not win in the end. Praise of God in His attributes. Hell is the goal of idolaters and polytheists. Patience enjoined upon Mohammad. The signs of God's might and the dire consequences of doubting it.

JONAH (x.) 87

Repudiation of sorcery. Signs of God's power, and the consequences of believing and disbelieving them. Insincerity of man: but former generations were destroyed for unbelief. Mohammad has no power to speak the Korān save as God reveals it. Idolatry ridiculed. Miracles disclaimed. Man believes when he is in danger, and disbelieves when he is rescued. The life of this world like grass that will be mown to-morrow. The reward of well and evil doing and the judgment of idolaters. God's might in creation. The Korān no forgery, as will be plainly seen one day. Every nation has its apostle and its appointed term, which cannot be hastened or retarded. Now the people are warned, and all they do is seen of God. God's power: He has no Son. The story of Noah and the ark, and Moses and the magicians, and the passage of the Red Sea, and the establishing of the Children of Israel. The people of Jonah. God compels unbelief or belief as He pleases, and none can believe without His permission. The signs of God are in the heavens and the earth. True worship.

THUNDER (xiii.) 104
The mighty works of God. The punishment of unbelief. Miracles disclaimed. The omniscience and unvariableness of God, the hurler of thunder and lightning and the giver of rain. The reward of the faithful; the torment of apostates. God misleads whom He will, and, if He pleased, could guide all mankind aright. Apostles have been mocked at before: and the mockers were punished. Paradise. Mohammad's task is only to warn: it is God's business to punish.

SPEECHES OF MEDINA 113

THE PERIOD OF HARANGUE. Aet. 53-63, A.D. 622-632 113

DECEPTION (lxiv.) 115
God's power in creation. Former apostles were rejected. The resurrection, though disbelieved, is a fact—a day when people shall find their hopes are deceptive. Paradise and Hell. All things are ordained by God. Obedience to God and the apostle enjoined. The pleasures of this world are to be distrusted, but the fear of God and almsgiving commendable.

TABLE OF CONTENTS.

                                                    PAGE

IRON (lvii.) 118

    Praise of God and exhortation to belief and almsgiving and fighting for the faith. The future state of the faithful and of the hypocrites. The charitable shall be doubly rewarded. The present life only a pastime and delusion. Everything predestined. The sending of the apostles, of Noah, Abraham, and Jesus. Asceticism repudiated. Exhortation to faith and fear.

THE VICTORY (xlviii.) 124

    A victory was given to encourage the faithful. Commendation of those who pledged themselves to support Mohammad and rebuke to the desert Arabs who held aloof (on the occasion of the expedition to Hudeybia); they shall not share in the spoil (of Khaibar). Promise of booty. The truce (of Hudeybia). The opposition to Mohammad's pilgrimage to Mekka shall be withdrawn; and a victory shall soon be won. The devotion of the faithful and their likeness.

HELP (cx.) 130

    Exhortation to praise God in the hour of triumph.

TABLE OF CONTENTS.   lxvii

PAGE

THE LAW GIVEN AT MEDINA . . 131

Religious Law 133

Creed and good works. Prayer. Alms. Fast. Pilgrimage. Fighting for the faith. Sacred month. Forbidden food. Oaths. Wine. Gambling. Statues. Divination.

Civil and Criminal Law . . . 139

Homicide; the blood-wit; murder; retaliation. Fighting against the faith. Theft. Usury. Marriage; adultery; divorce; slander. Testaments and heirs. Maintenance for widows. Testimony. Freeing slaves. Asylum. Small offences and great.

THE TABLE-TALK OF MOHAMMAD . 145

Of prayer 149
Of charity 151
Of fasting 153
Of reading the Korān 154
Of labour and profit 155
Of fighting for the faith 159
Of judgments 160
Of women and slaves 161
Of dumb animals 164
Of hospitality 165
Of government 166

TABLE OF CONTENTS.

	PAGE
Of vanities	168
Of death	172
Of the state after death	175
Of destiny	180
NOTES	183
Index of chapters of the Korān translated	196

THE SPEECHES AT MEKKA

I. THE POETIC PERIOD

Aet. 40-44

A.D. 609-613

THE NIGHT.

In the Name of God, the Compassionate, the Merciful.

BY the NIGHT when she spreadeth her veil,
By the DAY when it is manifested,
By what made the male and the female :
Verily your aims are diverse.

Then as for him who giveth alms and feareth God,
And putteth his faith in the Best,
We will speed him onward to ease.
And as for him who is covetous and desirous of riches,
And denieth the Best,
We will speed him onward to trouble ;
And his riches shall not avail him when he falleth down into Hell.
Verily ours is the guiding,
And ours the latter and the former life.

And I have warned you of a flaming fire :
None shall be burned in it but the wretch,
Who hath called it a lie and turned his back.

But the righteous shall be guided away from it—
He that giveth his substance in charity,
And doeth no man a kindness in hope of reward,
But only in seeking the face of his Lord the Most
    High ;
And in the end he shall surely be well pleased.

(xcii.)

THE COUNTRY.

In the Name of God, the Compassionate, the Merciful.

I SWEAR by this COUNTRY—
And thou art a dweller in this country—
And by father and child!
Verily we have created man amid trouble :—
Doth he think that no one shall prevail against him?
He saith "I have squandered riches in abundance:"
Doth he think that no one seeth him?
Have we not made him two eyes,
And a tongue and two lips,
And pointed him out the two highways?
Yet he doth not attempt the steep one.
And what shall teach thee what the steep one is?
The ransoming of captives,
Or feeding on the day of famine
The orphan of thy kindred
Or the poor that lieth in the dust;
Finally, to be of those who believe, and enjoin steadfastness on each other, and enjoin mercy on each other :—

These are the people of the right hand.
And those who disbelieve in our signs, they are the people of the left :
Over them a Fire closeth.

(xc.)

THE SMITING.

In the Name of God, the Compassionate, the Merciful.

THE SMITING! what is the Smiting?
And what shall teach thee what the Smiting is?
The Day when men shall be like scattered moths,
And the mountains like carded wool!
Then as for him whose scales are heavy—his shall be a life well-pleasing.
And as for him whose scales are light—his abode shall be the Bottomless Pit.
And what shall teach thee what that is?
A Raging Fire!

(ci.)

THE QUAKING.

In the Name of God, the Compassionate, the Merciful.

WHEN the earth shall quake with her QUAKING,
And when the earth hath cast forth her burdens,
And man shall say, "What aileth her?"
On that day shall she tell out her tidings,
Because thy Lord doth inspire her.
On that day shall men come in companies to behold their works,
And whosoever hath wrought an ant's weight of good shall behold it,
And whosoever hath wrought an ant's weight of evil shall behold it.

(xcix.)

THE RENDING ASUNDER.

In the Name of God, the Compassionate, the Merciful.

WHEN the Heaven is RENT ASUNDER,
And when the stars are scattered,
And when the seas are let loose,
And when the tombs are turned upside-down,
The soul shall know what it hath done and left undone.
O man! what hath deceived thee respecting thy Lord, the Generous;
Who created thee, and fashioned thee, and moulded thee aright?
In what form it pleased him He builded thee.
Nay! but ye take the Judgment for a lie!
But verily there are watchers over you—
Worthy reporters—
Knowing what ye do.
Verily the righteous shall be in delight,
And the wicked in Hell-Fire:
They shall be burnt at it on the day of doom,

And they shall not be hidden from it.
What shall teach thee what is the Day of Judgment?
Again, what shall teach thee what is the Day of Judgment?
A day when no soul can avail aught for another soul, for the ordering on that day is with God.

(lxxxii.)

THE CHARGERS.

In the Name of God, the Compassionate, the Merciful.

BY the CHARGERS that pant,
And the hoofs that strike fire,
And the scourers at dawn,
Who stir up the dust with it,
And cleave through a host with it!

Verily Man is thankless towards his Lord,
And verily he is witness thereof,
And verily in his love of weal he is grasping.
Doth he not know?—when what is in the tombs
    shall be laid open,
And what is in men's breasts shall be laid bare;
Verily on that day their Lord shall know them well!

(C.)

SUPPORT.

In the Name of God, the Compassionate, the Merciful.

WHAT thinkest thou of him who calleth the Day of
    Judgment a lie?
He it is who driveth away the orphan,
And is not urgent for the feeding of the poor.
Woe then to those who pray,
Those who are careless in their prayers,
Who make a pretence,
But withhold SUPPORT.

                              (cvii.)

THE BACKBITER.

In the Name of God, the Compassionate, the Merciful.

WOE to every BACKBITER, slanderer!
Who hath heaped up riches and counted them over!
He thinketh that his riches have made him everlasting:
Nay! he shall surely be cast into Blasting Hell.
And what shall teach thee what Blasting Hell is?
The fire of God kindled,
Which reaches over the hearts;
Verily it is closed over them [like a tent],
With stays well-stretched.

(civ.)

THE SPLENDOUR OF MORNING.

In the Name of God, the Compassionate, the Merciful.

BY the SPLENDOUR OF MORNING,
And the still of night!
Thy Lord hath not forsaken thee nor hated thee;
And the future will surely be better for thee than the present,
And thy Lord will surely give to thee and thou wilt be well pleased.
Did He not find thee an orphan and sheltered thee,
And found thee erring and guided thee,
And found thee poor and enriched thee?
Then as for the orphan, oppress him not,
And as for him who asketh of thee, chide him not away,
And as for the bounty of thy Lord, tell of it.

(xciii.)

THE MOST HIGH.

In the Name of God, the Compassionate, the Merciful.

MAGNIFY the name of thy LORD, THE MOST HIGH,
Who created, and fashioned,
And decreed, and guided,
Who bringeth forth the pasturage,
Then turneth it dry and brown.

We will make thee cry aloud, and thou shalt not forget,
Except what God pleaseth; verily He knoweth the plain and the hidden.
And we will speed thee to ease.
Admonish, therefore,—verily admonishing profiteth,—
Whoso feareth God will mind;
And there will turn away from it only the wretch
Who shall broil upon the mighty fire;
And then shall neither die therein, nor live.
Happy is he who purifieth himself,
And remembereth the name of his Lord, and prayeth.

But ye prefer the life of this world,
Though the life to come is better and more enduring.
Truly this is in the books of eld,
The books of Abraham and Moses.

(lxxxvii.)

THE WRAPPING.

In the Name of God, the Compassionate, the Merciful.

WHEN the sun shall be WRAPPED UP,
And when the stars shall fall down,
And when the mountains shall be removed,
And when the ten-month camels shall be neglected,
And when the wild beasts shall be huddled together,
And when the seas shall boil over,
And when souls shall be joined to their bodies,
And when the child that was buried alive shall be asked
For what crime she was slain;
And when the Books shall be laid open,
And when the sky shall be peeled off,
And when Hell shall be set a-blaze,
And when Paradise shall be brought near,—
The soul shall know what it hath wrought.

And I swear by the stars that hide,
That move swiftly and hide,
And by the darkening night,
And by the breath of dawn,—

Verily this is the word of a noble messenger,
Strong, firm in the favour of the Lord of the Throne,
Obeyed and trusted.
And your companion is not mad:
Of a surety he saw [the Angel] on the clear horizon:
And he is not mistrusted as to the unseen,
Nor is his the speech of a pelted devil.
Then whither go ye?
Verily this is but a Reminder to the worlds,
To whomsoever of you chooseth to walk aright:
But ye shall not choose it, except God choose it, the Lord of the worlds.

(lxxxi.)

THE NEWS.

In the Name of God, the Compassionate, the Merciful.

OF what do they question together?
Of the great NEWS,
About which they dispute?
Nay, but they shall know!
Again,—Nay, but they shall know!
Have we not made the earth as a bed?
And the mountains as tent-pegs?
And created you in pairs,
And made your sleep for rest,
And made the night for a mantle,
And made the day for bread-winning,
And built above you seven firmaments,
And put therein a burning lamp,
And sent down water pouring from the squeezed
    clouds
To bring forth grain and herb withal,
And gardens thick with trees?

Lo! the Day of Decision is appointed—
The day when there shall be a blowing of the
    trumpet, and ye shall come in troops,

And the heavens shall be opened, and be full of gates,
And the mountains shall be removed, and turn into mist.
Verily Hell lieth in wait,
The goal for rebels,
To abide therein for ages;
They shall not taste therein coolness nor drink,
Save scalding water and running sores,—
A meet reward!
Verily they did not expect the reckoning,
And they denied our signs with lies;
But everything have we recorded in a book:—
"Taste then: for we will only add torment to you."
Verily for the pious is a place of joy,
Gardens and vineyards,
And full-bosomed girls, their mates,
And a cup brimming over:
There shall they hear neither folly nor lying;—
A reward of thy Lord—a gift sufficient,
Of the Lord of the heavens and of the earth, and of what is between them, the Merciful!
They shall not obtain speech of him:—
On the day when the Spirit and the Angels shall stand in ranks, they shall have no utterance, save he to whom the Merciful shall give leave, and who speaketh rightly.

That is the day of truth ! Then he that chooseth,
    let him make for his Lord as his goal.
Verily we warn you of torment nigh at hand ;
On the day when man shall see what his hands
    have sent before him, and the unbeliever shall
    say, "Oh ! that I were dust."
(lxxviii.)

THE FACT.

In the Name of God, the Compassionate, the Merciful.

WHEN the FACT becomes fact,
None shall deny it is a fact,—
Abasing,—exalting!
When the earth shall be shaken in a shock,
And the mountains shall be powdered in powder,
And become like flying dust,
And ye shall be three kinds.

Then the people of the right hand—what people
    of good omen!
And the people of the left hand—what people of
    ill omen!
And the outstrippers, still outstripping :—
These are the nearest [to God],
In gardens of delight;
A crowd of the men of yore,
And a few of the latter days;
Upon inwrought couches,
Reclining thereon face to face.
Youths ever young shall go unto them round about

With goblets and ewers and a cup of flowing wine,—
Their heads shall not ache with it, neither shall they be confused;
And fruits of their choice,
And flesh of birds to their desire;
And damsels with bright eyes like hidden pearls,—
A reward for what they have wrought.
They shall hear no folly therein, nor any sin,
But only the greeting, " Peace! peace!"

And the people of the right hand—what people of good omen!
Amid thornless lote-trees,
And bananas laden with fruit,
And shade outspread,
And water flowing,
And fruit abundant,
Never failing, nor forbidden,
And wives exalted—
Verily we produced them specially
And made them virgins,
Amorous, of equal age,
For the people of the right hand,—
A crowd of the men of yore,
And a crowd of the latter days.

But the people of the left hand—what people of
    ill omen !—
Amid burning wind and scalding water,
And a shade of black smoke,
Not cool or grateful !
Verily, before that, they were prosperous ;
But they persisted in the most grievous sin,
And used to say,
" When we have died, and become dust and bones,
    shall we indeed be raised again,
And our fathers the men of yore ?"
Say : Verily those of yore and of the latter days
Shall surely be gathered to the trysting-place of a
    day which is known.
Then ye, O ye who err and call it a lie,
Shall surely eat of the tree of Zakkūm,
And fill your bellies with it,
And drink upon it scalding water,—
Drink like the thirsty camel :—
This shall be their entertainment on the Day of
    Judgment !

It is we who created you ; why then will ye not
    believe ?
Have ye considered the germs of life—
Is it ye who create them, or are we the creators?

It is we who have decreed death among you; yet are we not debarred
From changing you for your likes, or producing you how ye know not.
But ye have known the first creation: why will ye not mind?
Have ye considered what ye sow?
Is it ye who raise it, or are we the raisers thereof?
If we pleased we could surely make it dry, so that ye would stop and marvel, [saying]
" We have spent, yet we are forbidden [the fruits]."
Have ye considered the water ye drink?
Is it ye who send it down from the clouds, or do we send it down?
If we pleased we could make it salt; why will ye not be thankful?
Have ye considered the fire which ye kindle?
Is it ye who make the wood that produces it, or do we make it?
It is we who have made it for a reminder and a benefit to the traveller.
Then magnify the name of thy Lord the Most Great.

And I swear by the setting-places of the stars,
And that, if ye knew it, is verily a mighty oath,
Verily this is the honourable Korān,

Written in the preserved Book:
Let none touch it but the purified,—
A revelation from the Lord of the worlds.
Will ye then disdain this discourse,
And make it your daily bread to discredit it?
Why then when the dying man's soul has come up to his throat,
And ye at the moment are watching,—
And we are nearer to him than ye, although ye see us not,—
Why, if ye are to have no Judgment,
Do ye not cause that soul to return, if ye speak the truth?
But if he be one of those brought nearest to God,
There is rest for him and sweet odour and a garden of delights.
And if he be of the people of the right hand,
[He shall be greeted with] "Peace to thee," from the people of the right.
And if he be of those who call it a lie,
The erring,
Then an entertainment of scalding water,
And broiling in Hell.
Verily this is assured truth!
So magnify the name of thy Lord the Most Great.

(lvi.)

THE MERCIFUL.

In the Name of God, the Compassionate, the Merciful.

THE MERCIFUL hath taught the Korān;
He created man,
Taught him clear speech;
The sun and the moon in their courses,
And the plants and the trees do homage.
And the Heaven, He raised it, and appointed the balance.
(That ye should not transgress in the balance:—
But weigh ye justly and stint not the balance.)
And the Earth, He prepared it for living things,
Therein is fruit, and the palm with sheaths,
And grain with its husk, and the fragrant herb:
Then which of the bounties of your Lord will ye twain deny?
He created man of clay like a pot,
And He created the Jinn of clear fire:
Then which of the bounties of your Lord will ye twain deny?
Lord of the two Easts,
And Lord of the two Wests:
Then which of the bounties of your Lord will ye twain deny?

He has let loose the two seas which meet together;
Yet between them is a barrier they cannot pass:
Then which of the bounties of your Lord will ye twain deny?
He bringeth up therefrom pearls great and small:
Then which of the bounties of your Lord will ye twain deny?
And His are the ships towering on the sea like mountains:
Then which of the bounties of your Lord will ye twain deny?
All on the earth passeth away,
But the face of thy Lord abideth endued with majesty and honour:
Then which of the bounties of your Lord will ye twain deny?
All things in the Heaven and Earth supplicate Him, every day is He at work:
Then which of the bounties of your Lord will ye twain deny?
We will apply ourselves to you, O ye two notables:
Then which of the bounties of your Lord will ye twain deny?
O company of Jinn and men, if ye are able to compass the boundaries of the Heavens and of the Earth, then compass them; but ye shall not compass them, save in our might:

Then which of the bounties of your Lord will ye twain deny?

There shall be shot at you a flash of fire and molten brass; ye cannot defend yourselves:

Then which of the bounties of your Lord will ye twain deny?

And when the Heaven shall be rent and become rosy like a red hide:

Then which of the bounties of your Lord will ye twain deny?

On that day neither man nor Jinn shall be asked about their sin:

Then which of the bounties of your Lord will ye twain deny?

The sinners shall be known by their signs, and they shall be seized by the forelock and the feet:

Then which of the bounties of your Lord will ye twain deny?

"This is Hell which the sinners took for a lie,"

To and fro shall they wander between it and water scalding hot:

Then which of the bounties of your Lord will ye twain deny?

But for him who feareth the majesty of his Lord [shall be] two gardens:

Then which of the bounties of your Lord will ye twain deny?

With trees branched over:

Then which of the bounties of your Lord will ye twain deny?

And therein two flowing wells:

Then which of the bounties of your Lord will ye twain deny?

And therein of every fruit two kinds:

Then which of the bounties of your Lord will ye twain deny?

Reclining on couches with linings of brocade and the fruit of the gardens to their hand:

Then which of the bounties of your Lord will ye twain deny?

Therein the shy-eyed maidens neither man nor Jinn hath touched before:

Then which of the bounties of your Lord will ye twain deny?

Like rubies and pearls:

Then which of the bounties of your Lord will ye twain deny?

Shall the reward of good be aught but good?

Then which of the bounties of your Lord will ye twain deny?

And beside these shall be two other gardens:

Then which of the bounties of your Lord will ye twain deny?
Dark green in hue:
Then which of the bounties of your Lord will ye twain deny?
With gushing wells therein:
Then which of the bounties of your Lord will ye twain deny?
Therein fruit and palm and pomegranate:
Then which of the bounties of your Lord will ye twain deny?
Therein the best and comeliest maids:
Then which of the bounties of your Lord will ye twain deny?
Bright-eyed, kept in tents:
Then which of the bounties of your Lord will ye twain deny?
Man hath not touched them before, nor Jinn:
Then which of the bounties of your Lord will ye twain deny?
Reclining on green cushions and fine carpets:
Then which of the bounties of your Lord will ye twain deny?
Blessed be the name of thy Lord endued with majesty and honour.

(lv.)

THE UNITY.

In the Name of God, the Compassionate, the Merciful.

SAY: He is ONE God;
God the Eternal.
He begetteth not, nor is begotten;
Nor is there one like unto Him.

(cxii.)

THE FĀTIHAH.

In the Name of God, the Compassionate, the Merciful.

PRAISE be to God, the Lord of the Worlds!
The Compassionate, the Merciful!
King of the day of judgment!
Thee we worship, and Thee we ask for help.
Guide us in the straight way,
The way of those to whom Thou art gracious;
Not of those upon whom is Thy wrath nor of the erring.

(i.)

THE SPEECHES AT MEKKA

II. THE RHETORICAL PERIOD
Aet. 44-46
A.D. 613-615

THE KINGDOM.

In the Name of God, the Compassionate, the Merciful.

BLESSED be He in whose hand is the KINGDOM: and He is powerful over all;

Who created death and life to prove you which of you is best in actions, and He is the Mighty, the Very Forgiving;

Who hath created seven heavens in stages: thou seest no fault in the creation of the Merciful; but lift up thine eyes again; dost thou see any cracks?

Then lift up the eyes again twice; thy sight will recoil to thee dazzled and dim.

Moreover, we have decked the lower heaven with lamps, and have made them for pelting the devils, and we have prepared for them the torment of the flame.

And for those who disbelieve in their Lord, the torment of Hell: and evil the journey to it!

When they shall be cast into it, they shall hark to its braying as it boileth;—

It shall well-nigh burst with fury! Every time a troop is thrown into it, its keepers shall ask them, "Did not a warner come to you?"

They shall say, "Yea! a warner came to us; but

we took him for a liar, and said, 'God hath not sent down anything. Verily, ye are only in great error.'"

And they shall say, "Had we but hearkened or understood, we had not been among the people of the flame!"

And they will confess their sins: so a curse on the people of the flame!

Verily they who fear their Lord in secret, for them is forgiveness—a great reward.

And whether ye hide your speech, or say it aloud, verily He knoweth well the secrets of the breast!

What! shall He not know, who created? and He is the subtle, the well-aware!

It is He who hath made the earth smooth for you: so walk on its sides, and eat of what He hath provided—and unto Him shall be the resurrection.

Are ye sure that He who is in the Heaven will not make the earth sink with you? and behold, it shall quake!

Or are ye sure that He who is in the Heaven will not send against you a sand-storm,—so shall ye know about the warning!

And assuredly those who were before them called it a lie, and how was it with their denial?

Or do they not look up at the birds over their heads, flapping their wings? None supporteth them but the Merciful: verily He seeth all.

Who is it that will be a host for you, to defend you, if not the Merciful? verily the unbelievers are in naught but delusion!

Who is it that will provide for you, if He withhold His provision? Nay, they persist in pride and running away!

Is he, then, who goeth grovelling on his face better guided than he who goeth upright on a straight path?

Say: it is He who produced you and made you hearing and sight and heart—little are ye thankful!

Say: it is He who sowed you in the earth, and to Him shall ye be gathered.

But they say, "When shall this threat be, if ye are speakers of truth?"

Say: the knowledge thereof is with God alone, and I am naught but a plain warner.

But when they shall see it nigh, the countenance of those who disbelieved shall be evil,—and it shall be said, "This is what ye called for."

Say: Have ye considered—whether God destroy me and those with me, or whether we win mercy—still who will save the unbelievers from aching torment?

Say: He is the Merciful: we believe in Him, and in Him we put our trust—and ye shall soon know which it is that is in manifest error!

Say: Have ye considered if your waters should sink away to-morrow, who will bring you running water?

(lxvii.)

THE MOON.

In the Name of God, the Compassionate, the Merciful.

THE Hour approacheth and the MOON is cleft asunder.
But if they see a sign they turn aside, and say "Useless magic!"
And they call it a lie, and follow their own lusts:—but everything is ordained.
Yet there came to them messages of forbiddance—
Wisdom supreme—but warners serve not!
Then turn from them: the Day when the Summoner shall summon to a matter of trouble,
With eyes cast down shall they come forth from their graves, as if they were scattered locusts,
Hurrying headlong to the summoner: the unbelievers shall say, "This is a hard day!"

The people of Noah, before them, called it a lie, and they called our servant a liar, and said, "Mad!" and he was rejected.
Then he besought his Lord, "Verily I am overpowered: defend me."
So we opened the gates of heaven with water pouring forth,

And we made the earth break out in springs, and the waters met by an order foreordained;
And we carried him on a vessel of planks and nails,
Which sailed on beneath our eyes;—a reward for him who had been disbelieved.
And we left it as a sign; but doth any one mind?
And what was my torment and warning?
And we have made the Korān easy for reminding; but doth anyone mind?

Ad called it a lie; *but what was my torment and warning?*
Lo, we sent against them a biting wind on a day of settled ill-luck.
It tore men away as though they were trunks of palm-trees torn-up.
But what was my torment and warning?
And we have made the Korān easy for reminding; but doth any one mind?

Thamūd called the warning a lie:
And they said, "A single mortal from among ourselves shall we follow? verily then we should be in error and madness.
Is the reminding committed to him alone among us? Nay, he is an insolent liar."
They shall know to-morrow about the insolent liar!

Lo! we will send the she-camel to prove them: so mark them well, and be patient.
And predict to them that the water shall be divided between themselves and her, every draught taken in turn.
But they called their companion, and he took and hamstrung her—
And what was my torment and warning?
Lo! we sent against them one shout; and they became like the dry sticks of the hurdle-maker.
And we have made the Korān easy for reminding; but doth any one mind?

The people of Lot called the warning a lie;—
Lo! we sent a sand-storm against them, except the family of Lot, whom we delivered at daybreak
As a favour from us; thus do we reward the thankful.
And he had warned them of our attack, but they misdoubted the warning;
And they sought his guests, so we put out their eyes.
"*So taste ye my torment and warning!*"
And in the morning there overtook them a punishment abiding.
"*So taste my torment and warning.*"

*And we have made the Korān easy for reminding;
  but doth any one mind?*

And there came a warning to the people of Pharaoh:
They called our signs all a lie: so we gripped
  them with the grip of omnipotent might.

Are your unbelievers better men than those? Is
  there immunity for you in the Books?
Do they say, "We are a company able to defend
  itself?"
They shall all be routed, and turn their backs.
Nay, but the Hour is their threatened time, and
  the Hour shall be most grievous and bitter.
Verily the sinners are in error and madness!
One day they shall be dragged into the fire on
  their faces: "*Taste ye the touch of Hell.*"

Verily all things have we created by a decree,
And our command is but one moment, like the
  twinkling of an eye.
And we have destroyed the like of you:—*but doth
  any one mind?*
And everything that they do is in the Books;
Everything, little and great, is written down.
Verily the pious shall be amid gardens and rivers,
In the seat of truth, before the King Omnipotent.

(liv.)

K.

In the Name of God, the Compassionate, the Merciful.

K. By the glorious Korān.
Nay, they marvel that a warner from among themselves hath come to them: and the unbelievers say, "This is a marvellous thing!
When we are dead and are become dust!—that is a far-fetched return!"
We know what the earth consumeth of them, and with us is a book that keepeth count.
Nay, they called the truth a lie when it came to them, but they are in a perplexed state.
Will they not look up to the heaven above them, how we built it, and beautified it, and there are no flaws therein?
And we spread out the earth, and cast stable mountains upon it, and caused to grow there plants of all beauteous kinds,
For consideration and warning to every repentant servant.
And we sent down water from heaven as a blessing, and caused thereby gardens and harvest grain to grow,
And tall palm-trees with spathes heaped up,

A provision for our servants; and revived thereby a barren land. Like that shall the resurrection be.

Before them the people of Noah and the people of Er-Rass and Thamūd called the prophets liars,

And Ad, and Pharaoh, and the brethren of Lot, and the people of the grove, and the people of Tubba'—one and all called the apostles liars,—and found the threat true.

Were we then impotent as to the first creation? yet they are in doubt about a new creation.

We created man, and we know what his soul whispereth, and we are nearer to him than his jugular vein.

When the two note-takers take note, sitting on the right hand and on the left,

Not a word doth he utter, but a watcher is by him ready.

And the stupor of death shall come in truth;— "this is what thou would'st have avoided."

And the trumpet shall be blown,—that is the Day of the Threat!

And every soul shall come, along with a driver and a witness—

"Thou didst not heed this: so we have taken away from thee thy veil, and to-day thy sight is keen."

And his companion shall say, "This is what I am ready to witness."
"Cast ye into Hell every unbelieving rebel,
Hinderer of the good, transgressor, doubter,
Who setteth up other gods with God; cast ye him into the fierce torment."
His companion shall say, "O our Lord! I misled him not; but he was in fathomless error."
God shall say, "Wrangle not before me, for I charged you before about the threat.
My word does not change, and I am not unjust to my servants."
On that day will we say to Hell, "Art thou full?" and it shall say, "Is there more?"
And Paradise shall be brought nigh to the righteous, not afar:—
"This is what ye were promised, unto every one who turneth himself to God and keepeth His laws,
Who feareth the Merciful in secret, and cometh with a contrite heart;
Enter it in peace:"—that is the Day of Eternity!
They shall have what they please therein, and increase at our hands.

And how many generations have we destroyed before them, mightier than they in valour! then seek through the land—is there any refuge?

Verily in that is a warning to him who hath a heart, or giveth ear, and is a beholder.

And We created the heavens, and the earth, and what is between them, in six days, and no weariness touched us.

Then be patient with what they say, magnify thy Lord with praise before the rising of the sun and its setting,

And in the night magnify Him, and in the endings of the prayers.

And give ear to the day when the crier shall cry from a near place,

The day when they shall hear the shout in truth —that is the day of resurrection!

Verily it is we who give life and death, and to us do all return.

The day when the earth shall gape asunder over them suddenly—that is the gathering easy to us!

We know well what they say: and thou art not a tyrant over them.

But warn by the Korān him who feareth the threat.

(l.)

Y. S.

In the Name of God, the Compassionate, the Merciful.

Y. S. BY the wise Korān!
Verily thou art of the Messengers
Upon the straight way.
A revelation of the Mighty, the Merciful :—
To warn a people whose fathers were not warned, and themselves are heedless.
Our word has proved true against the most of them; yet they will not believe!
Verily we have put shackles on their necks, reaching to the chin, and their heads are tied back;
And we have put a barrier before them and a barrier behind them, and we have covered them so that they see not;
And it is all one to them whether thou warn them or warn them not: they will not believe.
Thou wilt only warn to good purpose him who followeth the monition and feareth the Merciful in secret: so tell him good tidings of forgiveness and a noble reward.
Verily it is we who quicken the dead, and write down the deeds they have sent before them and the vestiges they leave behind them;

and everything do we set down in the plain Exemplar.

And frame for them a parable—the people of the town [of Antioch], when the Apostles came to it;
When we sent unto them two, and they called them liars; so we strengthened them with a third, and they said, "Verily we are sent unto you."
The people said, "Ye are only men like us; and the Merciful hath not revealed aught; in sooth ye are only lying."
They said, "Our Lord knoweth that we are indeed sent unto you;
And there is naught laid upon us but to announce a plain message."
The people said, "Of a truth we have drawn an evil augury from you: unless ye desist, we will surely stone you, and a painful punishment shall surely betide you from us."
They said, "Your evil augury is with yourselves! If ye be warned?—Nay! ye are an ignorant people."
And there came from the furthest part of the city a man running: he said, "O my people! follow the Apostles,
Follow those who ask you not for recompense, and who are guided aright.

And what is in me, that I should not worship
   Him who made me and to whom ye must
   return ?
Shall I take gods beside Him ? If the Merciful
   be pleased to afflict me, their intercession will
   not avail me aught, nor will they deliver me ;
Verily in that case I should be in a manifest error.
Verily I believe in your Lord : therefore hear ye
   me."—
It was said, " Enter into Paradise," and he said,
   " Would that my people knew
How that my Lord hath forgiven me and hath made
   me one of the honoured !"
And afterwards we sent not down upon his people
   armies out of heaven nor what we were wont
   to send down :
It was but one shout, and lo, they were extinct !

O the pity of men ! No apostle cometh to them
   but they laugh him to scorn.
Do they not consider how many generations we
   have destroyed before them ?
Verily they shall not return to them,
But gathered together before us shall they all be
   arraigned.

And a sign for them is the dead earth which we

quicken and bring thereforth grain, and they eat of it;

And we make therein gardens of palm-trees and vines, and cause springs to gush forth therein;

That they may eat of its fruits, and of the labour of their hands: and will they not be thankful?

Extolled be the glory of Him who hath created all sorts of what the earth beareth, and of men's selves, and of that they know not of!

And a sign for them is the night. We draw away the day from it, and lo! they are in darkness;

And the sun hasteneth to her resting-place.—This is the ordinance of the Mighty, the Wise!—

And for the moon we have decreed his mansions, till he is wasted to the likeness of a withered palm-branch.

It is not meet that the sun should overtake the moon, nor the night outstrip the day; but each doth swim in its sphere.

And it is a sign for them that we carry their offspring in the burthened ship;

And that we create for them the like of it to ride on;

And if we please, we drown them, and there is no succour for them, nor are they delivered,

Save in our mercy, and for a transient joy.

And when it is said to them, " Fear what is before you and what is behind you; haply ye may obtain mercy : "

Thou bringest not one sign of the signs of their Lord but they turn away from it !

And when it is said to them, " Give alms of what God hath bestowed on you," they who disbelieve say to those who believe, " Shall we feed him whom God can feed if He pleases ? verily ye are only in manifest error."

And they say " When will this threat come to pass, if ye be speakers of truth ? "

They await but a single blast; it shall smite them whilst they are wrangling,

And they shall not be able to make their wills, and unto their families they shall not return.

And the trumpet shall be blown, and behold they shall hasten out of the graves to their Lord :

Saying, " Oh, woe is us ! who hath roused us from our sleeping-place ? This is what the Merciful threatened ; and the apostles spake truth."

There shall be but one blast, and, lo ! all are arraigned before us ;

And on that day no soul shall be wronged at all,

nor shall ye be recompensed save for what ye have wrought.

Verily on that day the people of Paradise shall be happy in their pursuits,
They and their wives reclining on couches in the shade;
They have fruit there and whatsoever they demand:
"Peace" is their greeting from a merciful Lord.

"Separate ye this day, O ye sinners!
Did I not charge you, O sons of Adam, not to serve the Devil,—surely he is your open enemy,—
But to worship Me: this is the straight way?
Yet he led away a great multitude of you: had ye no wits?
This is Hell, which ye were threatened with:
Roast there to-day, because ye did not believe."
On that day will we set a seal on their mouths, but their hands shall speak to us, and their feet shall bear witness of what they have earned for themselves.
And if we pleased, we could put out their eyes, and still would they hasten on their way: but how would they see?
And if we pleased we could transform them as they stand so that they could not go on or turn back;

And him whom we make old, we bow down his
 body: have they no wits?

We have not taught [Mohammad] poetry, nor
 would it befit him. It is only a warning and
 a plain Korān,
To warn whosoever liveth: and the sentence shall
 be carried out upon the unbelievers.
Do they not see that we have created for them, of
 what our hands have made, the cattle which
 they possess?
And we have subdued them unto them, and some
 of them are for riding and of some they eat,
And they have in them profit and milk to drink:
 and will they not be thankful?
But they have taken other gods beside God, if
 haply they may be holpen:
They are not able to help them; yet they themselves are an army arrayed for their defence.

But let not their speech grieve thee: verily, we
 know what they hide and what they show!
Doth not man see that we created him from a germ?
 Yet, behold he is an open adversary,
And he putteth arguments to us, and forgetteth his
 creation, saying, "Who can quicken bones that
 are rotten?"

Say : He who first made them to be shall quicken them : for all creating He knoweth well ;—
Who made for you fire from a green tree, and behold, ye kindle with it ;
And is not He who created the Heavens and the Earth able to create their like? Yea! for He is the wise Creator.
His command, when he willeth a thing, is only to say to it "BE," and it is !

Then extolled be the Perfection of Him in whose hand is the empire over all, and to whom ye must return.

(xxxvi.)

THE CHILDREN OF ISRAEL.

In the Name of God, the Compassionate, the Merciful.

EXTOLLED be the glory of Him who conveyed his servant by night from the Sacred Mosque to the furthest mosque, whose precincts we have blessed, to show him our signs ! Verily, He it is who heareth and seeth !

And we gave the Book of the Law to Moses and made it a guide to the CHILDREN OF ISRAEL —" Take ye no guardian beside Me,

Seed of those whom we bare [in the ark] with Noah ! Verily he was a grateful servant !"

And we ordained for the Children of Israel in the Book,—" Ye shall surely work iniquity in the earth twice, and ye shall be puffed up with a mighty arrogance."

So when the threat came to pass for the first of the two sins, we sent upon you servants of ours armed with grievous punishment ; and they went among your houses, and the threat was carried out.

Then in turn we gave you victory over them, and helped you with riches and sons, and made you a very numerous host.

If ye do well, ye will do well to your own souls, and if ye do ill, it will be to them also. And when the threat came to pass for the second sin,—[the enemy came] to afflict you, and to enter the mosque as they entered it the first time, and to utterly destroy what they had overpowered.

Haply your Lord will have mercy on you! and if ye turn, we will turn; but we have made Hell for a prison for the unbelievers.

Verily this Korān guideth to the right way and giveth good tidings to believers,

Who do that which is right, that for them is a great reward;

And that for those who believe not in the life to come, we have made ready an aching torment.

Man prayeth for evil as he prayeth for good: for man was ever hasty.

We have made the night and the day for two signs: then we blot out the sign of the night, and make the sign of the day manifest, that ye may seek bounty from your Lord, and may know the number of the years and the reckoning of time; and we have defined everything definitely.

And every man's fate we have fastened about his neck. And we will bring to him on the day of Resurrection a book which shall be offered to him open :—

"Read thy Book: thou thyself art accountant enough against thyself this day."

He who is guided, for his own good only shall he be guided, and he who erreth but to his own hurt; and one burthened soul shall not be burthened with another's burthen.

And we did not punish until we had sent an apostle.

And when we resolved to destroy a city, we enjoined its men of wealth, but they disobeyed therein; so the sentence proved true, and we destroyed it utterly.

How many generations have we swept away since Noah! and thy Lord knoweth and seeth enough of the sins of His servants.

Whoso desireth the present life, we will present him with what we please therein, to whom we choose: finally, we will make Hell for him to roast in, disgraced and banished:

But whoso desireth the life to come, and striveth after it strenuously, and he a believer,—the endeavour of these shall be acceptable:

To all, to these and those, will we extend the gifts of thy Lord; and the gifts of thy Lord are not limited.

See how we have made some of them excellent above others! but the life to come is greater in degrees and greater in excellence.

Set no other god with God, lest thou sit down disgraced and defenceless.

Thy Lord hath ordained that ye worship none but Him; and kindness to your parents, whether one or both of them attain old age with thee: then say not to them, "Fie!" neither reproach them; but speak to them generous words,

And droop the wing of humility to them out of compassion, and say, "Lord, have compassion on them, like as they fostered me when I was little."

(Your Lord knoweth perfectly what is in your souls, whether ye be well-doers;

And verily He is forgiving to the repentant.)

And render to thy kinsman his due, and to the poor and to the son of the road (but lavish not wastefully;

Truly the wasteful are brothers of the Devil, and the Devil is ungrateful to his Lord :)

But if thou turnest away from them, to seek the

mercy which thou hopest from thy Lord, yet speak to them gentle words.

And let not thy hand be chained to thy neck; nor yet stretch it forth right open, or thou wilt sit down in reproach and destitution.

Verily thy Lord will be openhanded with provision for whom He pleaseth, or He will be sparing; He knoweth and seeth His servants.

And slay not your children for fear of want: we will provide for them. Beware! verily killing them is a great sin.

And draw not near to inchastity; verily it is a foul thing, and evil is the course.

And slay not the soul whom God hath forbidden you to slay, unless for a just cause: and whosoever shall be slain wrongfully, we give his heir the right [of retaliation]; but let him not exceed in slaying; verily he is protected.

And approach not the substance of the orphan, except to make it better, till he cometh to maturity: and observe your covenants; verily covenants shall be inquired of hereafter.

And give full measure when ye measure, weigh with an even balance; that is best and fairest in the end.

And follow not that of which thou hast no knowledge: verily the hearing, and the sight, and the heart,—all of them shall be inquired of.

And walk not proudly on the earth: verily thou shalt never cleave the earth, nor reach to the mountains in height!

All that is evil in thy Lord's eye, an abomination.

That is part of the wisdom which thy Lord hath revealed to thee. And make no other god beside God, or thou wilt be thrown into Hell in reproach and banishment.

Hath then the Lord assigned to you sons, and shall He take for himself daughters from among the angels? verily ye do say a tremendous saying!

And we made variations in this Korān to warn them; yet it only increaseth their repulsion.

Say: If there were other gods with Him, as ye say, they would then seek occasion against the Lord of the throne.

Extolled be His glory, and be He greatly exalted far above what they say!

The seven heavens, and the earth, and all that is therein, magnify Him, and there is naught but magnifieth His praise; only ye understand not their worship. Verily He is forbearing, forgiving.

When thou declaimest the Korān, we put between

thee and those who believe not in the life to come a close veil;

And we put coverings over their hearts, lest they should understand it, and deafness in their ears.

And when thou tellest of thy Lord in the Korān as One, they turn their backs in repulsion.

We know well what they listen for, when they listen to thee, and when they whisper apart, when the wicked say, "Ye do but follow a man enchanted."

See what comparisons they make for thee! but they wander and cannot find the way.

They say, "What! when we have become bones and dust, shall we forsooth be raised as a new creature?"

Say: Yes! were ye stones, or iron, or any creature, the hardest [to raise again] that your minds can imagine. But they will say, "Who shall restore us?" Say: He who began you in the beginning! And they will wag their heads at thee and say, "When shall this be?" Say: Maybe it is nigh at hand.—

A day when God shall summon you and ye shall answer with His praise; and ye shall think that ye have tarried but a little while.

And say to my servants that they speak pleasantly: verily the Devil provoketh strife among them; verily the Devil is man's open enemy.

Your Lord knoweth you well; if He please He will have mercy on you; or if He please He will torment you; and we have not sent thee to be our governor over them!

Thy Lord knoweth well who is in the heavens and in the earth. And we distinguished some of the prophets above others, and we gave to David the Psalms.

Say: Call ye upon those whom ye profess beside Him; but they will have no power to put away trouble from you or alter it.

Those whom they invoke do themselves strive for access to their Lord, which of them shall be nearest: and they hope for His mercy and fear His torment: verily the torment of thy Lord is to be dreaded.

There is no city but we will destroy it before the Day of Resurrection, or torment it with grievous torment. That is written in the Book.

Nothing hindered our sending thee with signs but that the people of yore called them lies. We gave Thamūd the she-camel before their very eyes, but they maltreated her; and we send not [a prophet] with signs except to terrify.

And when we said to thee, "Verily thy Lord encompasseth mankind;"—and we made the vision which we showed thee, and the accursed tree in the Korān, only to prove men; and we will terrify them; but it shall only add to their great disobedience.

And when we said to the angels, "Bow down to Adam:" and they all bowed down save Iblīs: who said, "What! shall I bow down to him whom thou hast created of clay?"

And said, "Dost thou consider this one whom thou hast honoured above me? Verily, if thou didst spare me till the day of Resurrection, I would utterly destroy his offspring, all but a few!"

God said, "Begone; but whosoever of them followeth thee, verily, Hell is to be your reward—reward enough!

And tempt whom thou canst of them by thy voice; and assail them with thy horsemen and thy footmen, and share with them in their riches and their children, and make them promises. (But the Devil's promises are deceitful.)

Verily thou hast no power over my servants: and thy Lord sufficeth for a defender."

It is your Lord who driveth your ships on the sea, that ye may seek of His abundance, verily He is merciful to you.

And when a harm befalleth you at sea, they whom ye call on beside Him are missing! Then when He bringeth you safe to land, ye stand aloof: for man was ever thankless.

Are ye sure that He will not swallow you up on the shore, or send a sandstorm against you? then ye would not find for you any defender.

Or are ye sure that He will not turn you back again to sea, and send against you a storm of wind and drown you, because ye were thankless? Then shall ye find for yourselves no helper against us.

And we have honoured the sons of Adam; and we have borne them on the land and on the sea, and have fed them with good things, and distinguished them above many of our creatures.

On a day we will summon all men with their scripture: then whoso is given his book into his right hand,—these shall read their book and not be wronged a whit.

And he who has been blind in this life shall be blind in the life to come, and miss the road yet more.

And verily they had well-nigh tempted thee from what we revealed to thee, to forge against us something false; and then they would have taken thee to friend;

And had we not prevented thee, thou hadst well-nigh inclined to them a little:

In that case we would have made thee to taste of torment double in life and double in death, then should'st thou find for thyself no helper against us.

And they well-nigh frightened thee from the land, to drive thee out of it; but if they had, they should only have tarried a little while behind thee.

[This was our] custom with our apostles whom we sent before thee, and thou shalt find no changing in our custom.

Perform prayer from the setting of the sun till the fall of night, and the recital at dawn,—verily the recital at dawn is witnessed:

And watch thou part of the night as a voluntary service; it may be that thy Lord will raise thee to a place of praise:

And say: O my Lord, cause me to enter with a right entry, and to come forth with a right forthcoming, and grant me from thyself a power of defence.

And say: Truth is come and falsehood is fled away : verily falsehood is a fleeting thing.

And we send down from the Korān healing and mercy to the faithful ; but it shall only add to the ruin of the wicked.

And when we are gracious to man, he turneth away and standeth aloof; but when evil touches him he is in despair.

Say : Every one doeth after his own fashion, but your Lord knoweth perfectly who is best guided on the road.

And they will ask thee of the Spirit ; Say : The Spirit cometh at my Lord's behest, and ye are given but scant knowledge.

And assuredly, if we pleased we could take away what we have revealed to thee : then wouldst thou not find for thyself a defender against us,

Save in mercy from thy Lord ; verily His bounty towards thee is great.

Say : Surely if mankind and the Jinn united in order to produce the like of this Korān, they could not produce its like, though they helped one another.

We have varied every kind of parable for men in this Korān, but most men consent only to discredit it.

And they say, " We will by no means believe in thee till thou makest a spring to gush forth for us from the earth ;
Or till there cometh to thee a garden of palm-trees and grapes, and thou makest rivers to gush forth abundantly in its midst ;
Or thou make the heaven to fall down in pieces upon us, as thou pretendest ; or bring God and the angels before us ;
Or thou have a house of gold ; or thou ascend up into Heaven ; and we will not believe in thy ascent until thou send down to us a book which we may read." Say : Extolled be the glory of my Lord ! Am I aught save a man, a messenger ?
And nothing prevented men from believing, when the guidance came to them, but their saying, "Hath God sent a mere man as a messenger?"
Say : Had there been angels upon the earth walking at ease, we had surely sent them an angel from heaven as an apostle.
Say: God is witness enough between me and you: verily He knoweth and seeth His servants.
And whom God guideth, he is guided, and whom He misleadeth, thou shalt find him no protectors beside Him ; and we will gather them on the day of Resurrection upon their faces,

blind, and dumb, and deaf, hell is their abode; so oft as its fire dieth down, we will stir up the flame.

This is their reward, for that they believed not our signs, and said, "When we are become bones and dust, shall we indeed be raised a new creature?"

Do they not see that God, who created the heavens and the earth is able to create their likes? and He hath made an appointed term for them: there is no doubt of it; but the wicked consent only to deny it!

Say: If ye possessed the treasures of the mercy of thy Lord, ye would then assuredly keep them, in fear of spending: for man is niggardly.

Heretofore We brought to Moses nine evident signs: Ask then the Children of Israel [the story]—when he came unto them, and Pharaoh said unto him, "Verily I consider thee to be bewitched, O Moses."

He said, "Thou knowest that none hath sent these down as proofs but the Lord of the heavens and the earth; and verily I consider thee, O Pharaoh, accursed."

So he sought to drive them out of the land; but

we drowned him and those with him, every one.

And after this we said to the Children of Israel, "Dwell ye in the land, and when the promise of the life to come befalleth, we will bring you in a troop to judgment."

And in truth have we sent down [the Korān], and in truth came it down, and we have sent thee only to give good tidings and to warn.

And the Korān have we divided that thou mayest recite it unto men by degrees; and we have sent it down by [separate] sendings.

Say: Believe ye therein or believe ye not;—those verily to whom knowledge hath been given before, when it is told to them, fall down on their faces in adoration, and say, "Extolled be the glory of our Lord! verily the promise of our Lord is accomplished."

And they fall down upon their faces weeping, and it increaseth their humility.

Say: Call upon God, or call upon the Merciful, whichever ye call Him by; for His are the goodliest names. And be not loud in thy prayer, nor yet mutter it low; but follow a course between.

And Say: Praise be to God who hath not taken a son, and who hath no partner in the Kingdom, and no protector hath He for abasement; and glorify Him gloriously.

(xvii.)

THE SPEECHES AT MEKKA

III. THE ARGUMENTATIVE PERIOD

Aet. 46-53

A.D. 615-622

THE BELIEVER.

In the Name of God, the Compassionate, the Merciful.

H. M. THE revelation of the Book is from God the Mighty, the Wise,

Forgiver of sin, and accepter of repentance,—heavy in punishment,

Long-suffering: there is no God but He, to whom is your journeying.

None dispute about the signs of God save those who disbelieve; but let not their trafficking in the land deceive thee.

Before them the people of Noah, and the allies after them, denied, and every folk hath purposed against its apostle to overmaster him, and they argued with falsehood to rebut the truth therewith; but I did overmaster them and how great was my punishment!

And thus was the sentence of thy Lord accomplished upon those who disbelieved, that they should be inmates of the Fire!

They that bear the Throne and they that are round about it magnify the praise of their Lord and believe in Him and beg forgiveness for those who believe :—" O our Lord ! thou embracest all things in mercy and knowledge, give pardon to those who repent and follow thy path, and keep them from the torment of hell,

O our Lord, and bring them into the gardens of eternity which thou hast promised to them and to the just among their fathers and their wives and their offspring ; verily thou art the Mighty, the Wise ;

And keep them from evil ; for he whom thou keepest from evil on that day, on him hast thou had mercy—and that is the great prize !"

Verily to those who disbelieve shall come a voice, " Surely the hatred of God is greater than your hatred among yourselves, when ye are called to the faith, and disbelieve."

They shall say, " O our Lord, twice hast thou given us death, and twice hast thou given us life : and we acknowledge our sins : is there then a way to escape ?"—

" That hath befallen you because when one God was proclaimed, ye disbelieved : but when Partners were ascribed to Him, ye believed : but judgment belongeth unto God, the High, the Great."

It is He who showeth you His signs, and sendeth

down to you provision from heaven: but none mindeth except the repentant.

Then call on God with due obedience, though loth be the infidels;
Of high degree, Lord of the throne; He sendeth down the Spirit at His will upon whom He pleaseth of His servants to warn men of the day of the Tryst :—
The day when they shall come forth, and when nothing of theirs shall be hidden from God. Whose is the kingship on that day? It is God's, the One, the Conqueror!
The day every soul shall be rewarded for what it hath earned: no injustice shall there be on that day! Verily God is swift to reckon.
And warn them of the approaching Day, when their hearts shall choke in their throats,
When the wicked have no friend nor intercessor to prevail.
He knoweth the deceitful of eye, and what the breast concealeth,
And God judgeth with truth; but those gods whom they call on beside Him cannot judge aught. Verily it is God that heareth and seeth!

Have they not journeyed in the earth, and seen

what was the end of those who were before them? Those were mightier than they in strength, and in their footprints on the earth: but God overtook them in their sins, and there was none to keep them from God.

That was because apostles had come to them with manifestations, and they believed not: but God overtook them; verily He is strong and heavy in punishment.

We sent Moses of old with our signs and with plain authority,

To Pharaoh, and Haman, and Korah: and they said, "A lying wizard."

And when he came to them with truth from us they said, " Slay the sons of those who believe with them, and spare their women;" but the plot of the unbelievers was at fault:

And Pharaoh said, " Let me alone to kill Moses; and let him call upon his Lord: verily I fear lest he change your religion, or cause iniquity in the earth."

And Moses said, " Verily I take refuge with my Lord and your Lord from every one puffed up who believeth not in the day of reckoning."

And there spake a man of the family of Pharaoh, a BELIEVER, who concealed his faith, " Will ye kill a man because he saith my Lord is God, when he hath come unto you with manifestations from your Lord? for if he be a liar, upon him alone is his lie, but if he be a man of truth, somewhat of that which he threateneth will befall you. Verily God guideth not him who is an outrageous liar.

O my people, to-day is the kingdom yours who are uppermost in the earth! but who will defend us against the might of God if it come upon us?" Pharaoh said, "I will only show you what I think, and I will not guide you save in a right way."

Then said he who believed, "O my people, verily I fear for you the like of the day of the allies,

The like of the state of the people of Noah, and Ad, and Thamūd,

And of those who came after them; and God willeth not injustice to His servants.

And, O my people! verily I fear for you the day of crying out:

The day when ye shall turn your backs in flight, ye shall have no protector against God; and he whom God misleads, no guide has he.

Moreover, Joseph came unto you before with manifestations; but ye ceased not to doubt about [the message] he brought you, until when he died ye said, 'God will by no means send an apostle after him.' Thus God misleadeth him who is an outrageous doubter.

They who dispute about the signs of God, and no proof coming to them, are very hateful to God and to those who believe. Thus God sealeth the heart of all who are puffed up and arrogant."

And Pharaoh said, "O Haman, build me a tower, mayhap I shall reach the avenues,

The avenues of the heavens, and may ascend to the God of Moses: but verily I hold him a liar."

And thus the wickedness of his deed seemed good to Pharaoh, and he was turned away from the right path; but the plot of Pharaoh only came to ruin.

And he who believed said, "O my people, follow me: I will guide you the right way.

O my people, the life of this world is but a passing joy; but the life to come, that is the abode imperishable.

Whosoever doeth evil shall not be rewarded save with its like; and whosoever doeth right, whether male or female, being a believer—these shall enter paradise; and be provided therein without count.

And O my people! how is it that I bid you to salvation, but that ye bid me to the Fire?

Ye call me to disbelieve in God and join to Him that of which I have no knowledge: and I call you to the Mighty, the Very Forgiving.

There is no doubt but that those ye call me to are not to be called on in this world or in the world to come, and that we shall return unto God, and the transgressors shall be inmates of the Fire.

Then shall ye call to mind what I said to you: and I commit my case to God: verily God regardeth His servants."

So God kept him from the evil which they devised, and there encompassed the people of Pharaoh the woeful torment—

The Fire, to which they shall be exposed morning and evening; and on the day when the Hour cometh—" Enter, ye people of Pharaoh, into the sorest torment."

And when they shall wrangle together in the fire, the feeble shall say to those who were puffed up, "Verily we followed you: will ye then remove from us aught of the Fire?"

And those who were puffed up will say, "Verily we are all in it. Behold! God hath judged between His servants."

And they who are in the Fire shall say to the keepers of Hell, "Call on your Lord, that He remit us one day from the torment."

The keepers shall say, "Did there not come to you your apostles with manifestations?" They shall say, "Yea." The keepers shall say, "Call then," but the cry of the unbelievers shall be vain.

Verily we will help our apostles and those who believe, both in the life of this world and on the day when the witness shall stand forth;—

A day whereon the excuse of the wicked shall not profit them; but they shall have the curse and the abode of woe.

And of old gave we Moses the guidance, and the Children of Israel made we heirs of the Book,—a guidance and a warning to those who have understanding.

Be patient, therefore; verily the promise of God is true; and seek pardon for thy sins, and magnify the praises of thy Lord at eve and early morn.

Verily those who dispute about the signs of God, without proof reaching them, there is naught in their breasts but pride: and they shall not win. But seek refuge with God; verily, He heareth and seeth.

Surely the creation of the heavens and the earth is greater than the creation of man. But most men do not know.
Moreover the blind and the seeing are not equal, nor the sinner and they who believe and do the things that are right ;—little do they mind!
Verily the Hour is assuredly coming : there is no doubt of it ;—but most men do not believe.
And your Lord saith, "Call upon me ;—I will hearken unto you : but as to those who are too puffed up for my service, they shall enter Hell in contempt."

It is God who made you the night to rest in, and the day for seeing : verily God is bounteous to man, but most men are not thankful.
That is God your Lord, Creator of all things : there is no god but He : then why do ye turn away?
Thus do they turn away who gainsay the signs of God—
God, who made you the earth for a resting-place and the heaven for a tent, and formed you and made goodly your forms and provided you with good things—that is God, your Lord.
Then blessed be God, the Lord of the worlds!
He is the Living One. No god is there but He! then call upon Him, purifying your service to

Him. Praise be to God, the Lord of the worlds!

Say: Verily I am forbidden to serve those whom ye call on beside God, since there came to me manifestations from my Lord, and I am bidden to resign myself to the Lord of the worlds.

He it is who created you of dust, then of a germ, then of blood; then bringeth you forth a babe: then ye come to your strength, then ye become old men (but some of you die before) and reach the appointed term: haply ye will understand!

It is He who giveth life and death; and when He decreeth a thing, He only saith to it, "Be," and it is.

Hast thou not beheld those who cavil at the signs of God, how they are turned aside?

They who call the Book, and that with which we have sent our apostles, a lie: they shall soon know!

When the shackles shall be on their necks, and the chains, whilst they are dragged into Hell—then in the fire shall they be burned—

Then shall it be said to them, "Where is that which ye joined in worship beside God?" They shall say, "They are lost to us. Nay!

we did not call before upon anything." Thus God misleadeth the unbelievers.

" That is because ye exulted on earth in what was not true, and because ye were insolent.

Enter the gates of Hell to abide therein for ever: and wretched is the abode of the proud!

But be thou patient: verily the promise of God is true: and whether we show thee part of what we threatened them, or whether we make thee to die; yet to us shall they return.

We have sent apostles before thee. Of some we have told thee and of some we have not told thee: but no apostle was able to bring a sign unless by the permission of God. But when God's behest cometh, everything is decided with truth: and those perish who think it vain.

It is God who hath made for you the cattle, some to ride and some to eat,

(And ye have profit from them) and to attain by them the aims of your hearts, for on them and in ships are ye borne:

And He showeth you His signs: which then of the signs of God will ye deny?

Have they not journeyed in the earth, and seen what was the end of those who were before them? They were in number more than they, and mightier in strength, and in their footprints on the earth: but what they had earned availed them nothing;

And when their apostles came to them with manifestations, they exulted in what knowledge they had; but that which they had scoffed at encompassed them.

And when they beheld our might they said, "We believe in God alone, and we disbelieve in what we joined in worship with Him."

And naught availed their faith, after they witnessed our might. Such the way of God which was reserved for his servants—and therein the unbelievers have lost.

(xl.)

JONAH.

In the Name of God, the Compassionate, the Merciful.

A. L. R. THESE are the signs of the wise Book! Is it a matter of wonder to the people that we revealed to a man from among themselves, "Warn the people; and bring good tidings to those who believe, that the reward of their good faith is with their Lord?" The unbelievers say, "Lo! this is an evident sorcerer!"

Verily your Lord is God, who made the heavens and the earth in six days—then ascended the throne to govern all things: there is none to plead with Him save by His permission.—This is God, your Lord! then worship ye Him: will ye not mind?

Unto Him shall ye all return by the sure promise of God: behold! He produces a creature, then maketh it return again, that He may reward with equity those who believe and do the things that are right: but those who believe not, for them is the scalding drink, and an aching torment—because they did not believe.

It is He who hath made the sun for shining, and the moon for light, and ordained him mansions that ye may learn the number of years and the reckoning of time. God did not create that but in truth. He maketh His signs plain to a people who know.

Verily in the alterations of the night and the day, and in all that God created in the heavens and the earth, are signs to a godfearing folk.

Verily they who do not hope to meet us, and are satisfied with the life of this world, and are content with it, and they who are careless of our signs,—

Their dwelling-place is the Fire, for what they have earned.

Verily they who believe and do the things that are right, their Lord shall guide them because of their faith; beneath them rivers shall flow in gardens of delight:

Their cry therein shall be, "Extolled be thy glory, O God!" and their salutation therein shall be "Peace!"

And the end of their cry shall be, "Praise to God, Lord of the worlds!"

And if God should hasten woe upon men as they fain would hasten weal, verily their appointed term is decreed for them! therefore we leave those who hope not to meet us groping in their disobedience.

Moreover, when affliction toucheth man, he calleth us upon his side, sitting, or standing; and when we take away his affliction from him, he passeth on as though he had not called us in the affliction that touched him! Thus do the deeds of transgressors seem good to them!

We have destroyed generations before you, when they sinned and their apostles came to them with manifestations and they would not believe;—thus do we requite the sinful folk.

Then we made you their successors in the earth after them, to see how ye would act.

But when our manifest signs are recited to them, they who hope not to meet us say, " Bring a different Korān from this, or change it." Say: It is not for me to change it of mine own will. I follow only what is revealed to me: verily I fear if I disobey my Lord the torment of the great Day.

Say: If God pleased, I had not recited it to you nor taught it you; and already I had dwelt a lifetime amongst you before that: have ye then no wits?

And who is more wicked than he who forgeth a lie

against God, or saith His signs are lies? Surely the sinners shall not prosper!

And they worship beside God that which cannot hurt them or help them; and they say, "These shall be our pleaders with God." Say: Will ye tell God of anything He doth not know in the heavens and in the earth? Extolled be His glory! and far be He above what they associate with Him!

Men were of only one religion: then they differed, and had not a decree gone forth from thy Lord, there had certainly been made a decision between them of that whereon they differed.

And they say, "Had a sign been sent down to him from his Lord . . ."—but say: The unseen is with God alone: wait, therefore; verily I am waiting with you.

And when we caused men to taste of mercy after affliction had touched them, behold! they have a plot against our signs! Say: God is quick at plotting! verily our messengers write down what ye plot.

He it is who maketh you journey by land and sea, until, when ye are in ships—and they run with them before a fair wind, and they rejoice thereat, there cometh upon them a violent wind, and the waves come upon them from every side, and they suppose they are sore pressed therewith; they call on God, offering Him sincere religion :—" Do thou but deliver us from this, and we will indeed be of the thankful."

But when we have delivered them, lo, they transgress unjustly on the earth! O ye people! ye wrong your own souls only for the enjoyment of the life of this world: then to us shall ye return; and we will tell you what ye have done.

The likeness of the life of this world is as the water which we send down from the heaven, and there mingleth with it the produce of the earth of which men and cattle eat, until when the earth hath put on its blazonry and is arrayed, and its inhabitants think it is they who ordain it, our command cometh to it by night or day, and we make it mown down, as if it had not teemed yesterday! Thus do we explain our signs to a reflecting folk.

And God calleth you unto the abode of peace: and guideth whom He will into the straight way:

To those who have done well, weal and to spare,
Neither blackness shall cover their faces nor shame! these are the inmates of Paradise, to abide therein for ever.
And as for those who have earned evil, the recompense of evil is its like; shame shall cover them—no defender shall they have against God—as though their faces were darkened with the gloom of night: these are the inmates of the Fire to abide therein for ever.
And on the day we will gather them all together, then will we say to those who made Partners with God, "To your place, ye and your Partners!" and we will separate between them; and their partners shall say, "Ye worshipped not us,
And God is witness enough between us and you that we were indifferent to your worship!"
Then shall every soul make proof of what it hath sent on before, and they shall be brought back to God their true Master, and what they devised shall vanish from them.

Say: Who provideth you from the heaven and the earth? who is king over hearing and sight? and who bringeth forth the living from the dead and bringeth forth the dead from the

JONAH.

living? and who ruleth all things? And they shall say, "God:" then say: Do ye not fear?

So that is God your true Lord: and after the truth, what is there but error? How then are ye turned away?

Thus is the word of thy Lord fulfilled upon those who work iniquity: they shall not believe.

Say: Is there any of the Partners [of God] who can produce a creature, then bring it back again? Say: God produceth a creature then bringeth it back again: how then are ye deceived?

Say: Is there any of the Partners who guideth to the truth? Say: God guideth unto the truth. Is he who guideth to the truth the worthier to be followed, or he who guideth not except he be guided? What is in you so to judge?

And most of them only follow a fancy: but a fancy profiteth nothing against the truth! verily God knoweth what they do.

Moreover this Korān could not have been devised without God: but it confirmeth what preceded it, and explaineth the Scripture—there is no doubt therein—from the Lord of the worlds.

Do they say, "He hath devised it himself?"

Say: Then bring a chapter like it: and call on whom ye can beside God, if ye be speakers of truth.

Nay, they call all that a lie, of which they compass not the knowledge, though the explanation of it hath not yet been given them; so did those who were before them call the Scriptures lies: but see what was the end of the wicked!

And some of them believe in it, and some of them believe not in it. But thy Lord knoweth best about the evildoers.

And if they call thee a liar, say, I have my work, and ye have your work: ye are clear of what I work, and I am clear of what ye work.

And some of them hearken to thee; but canst thou make the deaf hear if they have no wits?

And some of them regard thee; but canst thou guide the blind when they see not?

Verily God doth not wrong man a whit, but men wrong themselves.

And on a day He will gather them, as though they had tarried but an hour of the day: they shall know one another! They are lost who denied the meeting with God and were not guided!

Whether we show thee part of what we threatened

against them, or whether we take thee to ourself [before], to us is their return—then shall God be witness of what they have done.

And every nation hath its apostle; and when their apostle is come, it is decided between them with equity, and they are not wronged.

Yet they say, " When will this promise be, if ye be speakers of truth ? "

Say: I have no power for myself for woe or weal, except as God pleaseth. Every people hath its appointed term: when their term is come, they shall not put it off nor hasten it an hour.

Say: Bethink ye, if the torment of God come upon you by night or by day, what portion of it will the sinners willingly hasten on?

When it happeneth, will ye believe it then? Yet would ye fain hasten it on!

Then shall it be said to those who transgressed, " Taste ye the torment of eternity! Shall ye be rewarded save according to what ye have earned ? "

They would fain know of thee if this is true. Say: Yea, by my Lord, it is indeed true, and ye cannot weaken Him.

And if every soul that transgressed owned all that is on earth, he would assuredly give it in ransom; and they will declare their repentance when they have seen the torment: and there shall be a decision between them with equity, and they shall not be wronged.

Is not indeed whatsoever is in the heavens and the earth God's? Is not indeed the promise of God true? But most of them do not know!

He giveth life and death, and to Him shall ye return.

O ye people! now hath a warning come to you from your Lord, and a healing for what is in your breasts, and a guidance and a mercy to the believers.

Say: By the grace of God and his mercy! And in that let them therefore rejoice: this is better than what they heap up.

Say: Do ye consider what God hath sent down to you for provision: but ye made thereof unlawful and lawful? Say, did God permit you? or do ye forge against God?

But what will they think on the day of resurrection who forge a lie against God? Truly God is full of bounty towards man; but most of them are not thankful.

Thou shalt not be in any business, and thou shalt not read from the Korān, and ye shall not do any deed, but we are witness against you when ye are engaged therein ; and there escapeth not thy Lord an ant's weight in earth or in heaven : and there is nothing lesser or greater than that, but it is in the plain Book.

Are not they truly the friends of God on whom is no fear neither are they sorrowful—

They who believed and feared God,—

For them are good tidings in the life of this world, and in the life to come there is no changing in God's sentences. That is the great prize !

And let not their discourse grieve thee : verily all power belongeth to God, He it is who heareth and knoweth.

Doth not whoever is in the heavens and whoever is in the earth belong to God ? then what do they follow who call upon Partners beside God ? verily they follow but a fancy ; and verily they are naught but liars.

It is He who made you the night to rest in, and the day for seeing : verily in that are signs to a folk that can hear !

They say, " God hath taken him a son." Extolled be his glory ! He is the Self-sufficient, all that is in the heavens, and all that is in the

earth is his! ye have no warranty for this! do ye say about God that which ye know not?"
Say: Verily they who forge this lie against God shall not prosper:—
A passing joy in this world, then to us they return; and then we will make them taste the grievous torment, because they did not believe.

And tell them the story of Noah, when he said to his people,—" O my people! though my dwelling with you and my warning you of the signs of God hath been grievous to you, yet in God do I put my trust: so gather together your case and your Partners; then will not your case fall upon you in the dark: then decide about me and delay not.
And if ye turn, yet ask I no reward from you: my reward is with God alone, and I am commanded to be of those who are resigned."
But they called him a liar, so we delivered him and those who were with him in the ship, and we made them to survive; and we drowned those who had called our signs lies: see then what was the end of those who were warned!

Then after him, we sent apostles to their people,

and they came to them with manifestations: but they would not believe in what they had denied before: thus do we put a seal upon the hearts of the transgressors.

Then sent we, after them, Moses and Aaron to Pharaoh and his nobles with our signs; but they were puffed up and were a sinful folk.

And when the truth came to them from us, they said, "This is clear sorcery indeed."

Moses said, "Say ye of the truth when it is come to you, Is this sorcery?—but sorcerers shall not prosper."

They said, "Art thou come to us to hinder us from what we found our fathers in, and in order that for you twain there shall be majesty in the land? but we are not going to believe in you!"

And Pharaoh said, "Fetch me every wise sorcerer." And when the sorcerers came, Moses said to them, "Cast down what ye have to cast."

And when they had cast them down, Moses said, "What ye come with is sorcery: verily God will make it vain; aye, God doth not prosper the work of evildoers;

And God will establish the truth by his word, though loth be the sinners."

And none believed in Moses but the children of his own folk, for fear of Pharaoh and his nobles, lest he should afflict them: for of a truth Pharaoh was mighty in the earth, and verily he was of the transgressors.

And Moses said, "O my people! if ye believe in God, put your trust in Him, if ye are resigned."

And they said, "In God do we put our trust. O our Lord, make us not a trial to the folk of the wicked,

And deliver us in Thy mercy from the folk of the unbelievers."

Then revealed we to Moses and to his brother: "Build houses for your people in Egypt, and make your houses with a Kibla, and perform prayer, and give good tidings to the believers."

And Moses said, "O our Lord, thou hast indeed given to Pharaoh and his nobles adornments and riches in the life of this world: O our Lord! may they err from thy way; O our Lord, confound their riches, and harden their hearts, so shall they not believe until they see the aching torment."

God said: "Your prayer is heard, then stand ye upright, and follow not the path of those who know not."

And we brought the Children of Israel across the

JONAH.

sea; and Pharaoh and his host followed them, eager and hostile, until when drowning overtook him he said, "I believe that there is no God but He in whom the Children of Israel believe, and I am one of the resigned."

"Now! thou hast been rebellious aforetime, and wast one of the evildoers,

This day will we raise thee in thy flesh, to be a sign to those who come after thee: but verily many men are heedless of our signs!"

Moreover we lodged the Children of Israel in a firm abode, and provided them with good things: and they did not differ until the knowledge came to them; verily thy Lord will decide between them on the Day of Resurrection concerning that on which they differed.

And if thou art in doubt of what we have sent down to thee, inquire of those who read the Scriptures before thee. Now hath truth come unto thee from thy Lord: then be not thou of those who doubt,

Neither be of those who deny the signs of God lest thou be among the losers.

Verily they against whom the word of thy Lord is passed shall not believe,—

Though there came unto them every kind of sign,
—till they behold the aching torment.
Else any city had believed, and its faith had benefited it :—save the people of JONAH; when they believed, we took away from them the torment of shame in the life of this world, and provided for them awhile.
But if thy Lord pleased, verily all who are in the earth had believed together. Then canst thou compel men to become believers?
It is not in a soul to believe but by the permission of God : and He shall lay His curse on those who have no wits.
Say : Look upon that which is in the heavens and in the earth : but signs and warners avail not a folk that will not believe!
What then can they expect but the like of the days of those who passed away before them?
Say : Wait ye,—I too am waiting with you.
Then will we deliver our apostles and those who believe : thus is it binding on us to deliver the faithful.
Say : O ye people! if ye are in doubt of my religion, I do not worship those whom ye worship beside God; but I worship God, who taketh you away; and I am commanded to be of the faithful.

And set thy face towards religion as a Hanîf, and be not of those idolaters:

And invoke not beside God that which can neither help nor hurt; for if thou do, thou wilt certainly be of the wicked.

And if God touch thee with affliction, there is none to remove it but He. And if He desire thy good, there is none to hinder His bounty—He will confer it on whom He pleaseth of his servants: and He is the Forgiving, the Merciful!

Say: O ye people! now hath truth come unto you from your Lord; then he who is guided, is guided only for his own behoof: but he who erreth doth err only against himself; and I am no governor over you!

And follow what is revealed to thee: and be patient till God judgeth; and He is the best of judges.

(x.)

THE THUNDER.

In the Name of God, the Compassionate, the Merciful.

A. L. M. R. THESE are the Signs of the Book! and that which was sent down to thee from thy Lord is the truth: but most men do not believe.

It is God who raised the heavens without pillars that ye can see; then ascended the Throne, and subdued the sun and the moon: each runneth to its appointed goal, to rule every thing, to manifest signs. Haply ye will be convinced of meeting your Lord!

And it is He who spread out the earth, and put thereon firm mountains, and rivers; and of every fruit He hath made therein two kinds: He maketh the night to cover the day; verily in that are signs for reflecting folk.

And on the earth are neighbouring tracts, and gardens of grapes, and corn, and palms clustered and not clustered at the root; they are watered by the same water, yet we make some better than others for food: verily in that are signs for folk that have wits.

If ever thou dost wonder, wonderful is their saying, "What! when we have become dust, shall we indeed become a new creation?"

These are they who disbelieve in their Lord: and these shall have the shackles on their necks, and these shall be the inmates of the fire to abide therein for ever.

They will bid thee hasten evil rather than good: examples have passed away before them; and verily thy Lord is full of forgiveness unto men despite their iniquity; and verily thy Lord is heavy in punishing.

And they who disbelieve say, "Unless a sign be sent down to him from his Lord . . ." Thou art but a warner, and to every people its guide.

God knoweth what every woman beareth, and the decrease of the wombs and the increase; for the pattern of all things is with Him,

Who knoweth the hidden and the seen, the Great, the Most High.

Equal is he of you who concealeth his words and he that proclaimeth them: he who hideth by night, and he who goeth abroad by day.

Each hath angels before him and behind him, who watch over him by God's command. Verily God doth not change towards a people, till they change themselves; and when God willeth evil unto a people, there is no averting it, nor have they any protector beside Him.

It is He who showeth you the lightning for fear and hope [of rain], and gathereth the lowering clouds,

And the THUNDER magnifieth His praise, and the angels, for awe of Him, and He sendeth His thunderbolts and smiteth therewith whom He pleaseth:—and they are wrangling about God! but strong is His might!

Unto Him is the true cry: but those whom they cry to beside Him shall answer them naught save as one who stretcheth forth his hands to the water that it may reach his mouth, but it doth not reach it! The cry of the unbelievers is but in error.

And unto God bow down all things in the heavens and the earth, willingly or unwillingly, and their shadows at morn and eve!

Say: Who is Lord of the heavens and the earth? Say: God. Say: Why then have ye taken beside Him Patrons who are powerless for weal or woe to themselves? Say: What! are the blind and the seeing alike? or are darkness and light the same? or have they made Partners for God, who create as He creates, so that they confuse the creation? Say: God is the Creator of all things, He is the One, the Conqueror.

He sendeth down water from heaven; and the valleys flow in their degree, and the torrent beareth along foaming froth, and from the [ore] which they burn in the fire, desiring ornaments or necessaries, a scum like it ariseth. So doth God liken truth and falsehood. As to the scum it passeth off as refuse, and as to what profiteth man it remaineth on the earth. Thus doth God frame parables. For those who respond to their Lord, good; but those who respond not to Him, had they all that the earth containeth and its like beside it, they would surely give it in ransom: these shall have an evil reckoning, and Hell shall be their home,— and wretched the bed!

Is he who knoweth that what hath been sent down to thee from thy Lord is naught but the truth, like to him who is blind? but men of understanding alone will mind,

Who fulfil their covenant with God and break not the compact;

And who join what God hath bidden to be joined, and who fear their Lord and dread the evil reckoning;

And who are patient, seeking the face of their Lord, and perform prayer and give alms secretly and openly of what we have provided them, and turn away evil with good: for these is the reward of the Abode,—

Gardens of eternity, into which they shall enter together with those who were just of their fathers and their wives and their offspring: and the angels shall go in unto them at every gate [saying]:—

"Peace be upon you! because ye were patient." And pleasant is the reward of the Abode!

But those who break God's covenant after they have pledged it, and cut asunder what God hath bidden to be joined, and work iniquity in the earth, for these is a curse and a sore abode!

God is lavish with provision to whom He pleaseth, or He stinteth it. And they rejoice in the life of this world; but the life of this world is but a passing joy to the life to come.

And they who disbelieve say, "Unless a sign be sent down to him from his Lord. . ." Say:

God truly misleadeth whom He will; and He guideth to himself those who repent,

Who believe, and whose hearts are at peace in the remembrance of God! yea, in the remembrance of God shall the hearts be at peace of those who believe and do the things that are right—good betide them, and happy be their goal!

Thus have we sent thee among a nation, before whom other nations have passed away, that thou mayest tell them what we have inspired thee with: yet they disbelieve in the Merciful! Say: He is my Lord—there is no God but Him. In Him do I put my trust, and unto Him is my return.

Though there were a Korān by which the mountains were removed or the earth cloven or the dead given speech—Nay! to God belongeth the rule in all: know not they who believe, that if God pleased, He would certainly have guided men in all?

And calamity shall not cease to befal the unbelievers for what they have done, or settle hard by their dwellings, until the promise of God shall come to pass. Verily God will not fail in what He promised.

Before thee apostles have been mocked at—and long I suffered those who disbelieved; then I took hold of them; and how great was my punishment!

Who then is he that is standing over every soul to mark what it hath earned? Yet they made Partners with God! Say: Name them! could ye inform him of what He knoweth not in the earth, or are they aught beyond words? Nay, their artifice commended itself to those who disbelieve; and they are turned aside from the road; and whom God misleadeth, he hath no guide.

Torment is theirs in the life of this world, and assuredly the torment of the world to come shall be worse, and they shall have no one to ward them from God.

A likeness of the Paradise which is promised to those that fear God:—The rivers flow beneath it; its food and its shades are everlasting. That is the end of those who fear God: but the end of the unbelievers is the Fire.

They to whom we have given the Book rejoice in what hath been sent down to thee, yet some of the confederates deny a part of it. Say:

I am commanded only to worship God, and not to associate any with Him: on Him I cry, and unto Him is my goal.

Thus have we sent down the Korān as an Arabic judgment; and assuredly, if thou followed their desires after the knowledge had come to thee, thou shouldst have no protector nor warder against God.

And we have sent apostles before thee, and gave them wives and offspring. But to no apostle was it given to bring a sign save by God's permission: to each age its Book.

God wipeth out or confirmeth what He pleaseth, and with Him is the Mother of the Book.

And whether we show thee somewhat of that which we promised them, or take thee hence before; verily, it is thine to announce only, and ours to take account.

See they not that we come into the land and cut down its chiefs? And when God judgeth, there is none to reverse His sentence: and He is swift to reckon.

And those who were before them plotted: but God's is the master plot: He knoweth what every one soul earneth, and the infidels shall know for whom is the reward of the abode.

And those who disbelieve shall say, "Thou art not sent from God." Say: God is witness enough between me and you, and he that hath knowledge of the Book.

(xiii.)

THE SPEECHES OF MEDINA

THE PERIOD OF HARANGUE
Aet. 53-63
A.H. 1-11 = A.D. 622-632

I

DECEPTION.

In the Name of God, the Compassionate, the Merciful.

ALL that is in the heavens, and all that is in the earth, magnifieth God: His is the kingdom, His is the praise, and He is powerful over all things.

It is He who hath created you; and one of you is an unbeliever, and another a believer; and God seeth what ye do.

He created the heavens and the earth in truth; and He hath fashioned you and made goodly your forms; and to Him is your journeying.

He knoweth what is in the heavens and the earth; and He knoweth what ye hide and what ye manifest; and God knoweth well the secrets of the breast.

Hath not the story come to you of those who disbelieved aforetime, and tasted the evil fruit of their doings, and received an aching torment?

That was because when their apostles had come to them with manifestations, they said, "Shall mortal men guide us?" And they believed not and turned their backs. But God had no need of them; and God is Self-sufficient and worthy to be praised!

The unbelievers pretend that they shall by no means be raised again. Say: Nay, by my Lord, but ye shall be raised; then shall ye certainly be told of what ye have done: and that is easy with God.

Believe then in God and His Apostle, and in the light which we have sent down; for God knoweth perfectly what ye do.

The day when He shall gather you together for the Day of Assembly, that is the day of DECEPTION. And whoso believeth in God and doeth that which is right, God shall take away his sins, and He will bring him into the gardens beneath which rivers flow, to dwell there evermore: that is the great prize!

But those who believe not, but deny our signs—those shall be the inmates of the fire, to dwell therein for ever; and evil is their journey.

There happeneth no misfortune but by God's permission; and whoso believeth in God, He guideth his heart; and God knoweth all things.

DECEPTION.

Obey God, therefore, and obey the Apostle : but if ye turn away, our Apostle is only charged with a plain message :—

God, there is no God but He! Then in God let the faithful trust.

O ye who believe! verily in your wives and your children ye have an adversary, wherefore beware of them. But if ye relent and pardon and forgive, then verily God too is Forgiving and Merciful.

Your wealth and your children are but a snare : but God, with Him is the great reward.

Then fear God with all your might, and hear and obey, and give alms for your own sakes ; and whoso is saved from his own covetousness,— these it is who prosper.

If ye lend God a good loan, He will double it to you, and will forgive you : for God is Grateful, Mild,

Knowing the secret and the open ; the Mighty, the Wise!

(lxiv.)

IRON.

In the Name of God, the Compassionate, the Merciful.

ALL that is in the heavens and the earth magnifieth God, and He is the Mighty, the Wise.

His is the kingdom of the heavens and the earth, He giveth life and giveth death, and He is powerful over all things.

He is the first and the last, the seen and the unseen, and all things doth He know.

It is He who created the heavens and the earth in six days, then ascended the Throne; He knoweth what goeth into the earth and what cometh out of it, and what cometh down from the sky and what riseth up into it; and He is with you, wherever ye be; and God seeth what ye do.

His is the kingdom of the heavens and the earth, and to God shall all things return.

He maketh the night to follow the day, and He maketh the day to follow the night, and He knoweth the secrets of the breast.

Believe in God and His apostle, and give alms of

what He hath made you to inherit; for to those of you who believe and give alms shall be a great reward.

What aileth you that ye do not believe in God and His Apostle who calleth you to believe in your Lord? He hath already accepted your covenant if ye believe.

It is He who hath sent down to His servant manifest signs to lead you from darkness into light: for God is indeed kind and merciful towards you.

And what aileth you that ye give not alms in the path of God, when God's is the heritage of the heavens and the earth? Those of you who give before the victory, and fight, shall not be deemed equal,—they are of nobler degree than those who give afterwards and fight. Yet to all hath God promised the beauteous reward; and God knoweth what ye do.

Who is he who will lend God a good loan?—He will double it for him, and his shall be a noble recompense.

The day ye shall see the faithful, men and women, their light running in front and on their right hand—" Glad tidings for you this day!—

gardens whereunder rivers flow, to abide therein for ever:" that is the great prize!

The day when the hypocrites, men and women, will say to those who believe, "Stay for us, that we may kindle our light from yours." It shall be said, "Go back and find a light." And there shall be set up between them a wall, with a gate in it; and inside, within it, shall be Mercy, and outside, in front of it, Torment! They shall cry out, "Were we not with you?" The others shall say, "Yea! but ye fell into temptation, and waited, and doubted, and your desires deceived you, till the behest of God came,—and the arch-tempter beguiled you from God."

And on that day no ransom shall be accepted from you, nor from those who disbelieved—your goal is the Fire, which is your master; and evil is the journey thereto.

Hath not the Hour come to those who believe, to humble their hearts to the warning of God and the truth which He hath sent down? and that they may not be like those who received the Scripture aforetime, whose lives were prolonged, but their hearts were hardened, and many of them were disobedient.

Know that God quickeneth the earth after its

death : now have we made clear to you the signs,—haply ye have wits !

Verily the charitable, both men and women, and they who lend God a good loan, it shall be doubled to them, and theirs shall be a noble recompense.

And they who believe in God and His Apostle, these are the truth-tellers and the witnesses before their Lord : they have their reward and their light. And they who disbelieve and deny our signs—these are the inmates of Hell !

Know that the life of this world is but a game and pastime and show and boast among you; and multiplying riches and children is like rain, whose vegetation delighteth the infidels —then they wither away, and thou seest them all yellow, and they become chaff. And in the life to come is grievous torment,

Or else forgiveness from God and His approval : but the life of this world is naught but a delusive joy.

Strive together for forgiveness from your Lord and Paradise, whose width is as the width of heaven and earth, prepared for those who believe in God and in His Apostle. That is the grace of God ! who giveth it to whom He pleaseth; and God is the fount of boundless grace.

There happeneth no misfortune on the earth or to yourselves, but it is written in the Book before we created it: verily that is easy to God!—

That ye may not grieve over what is beyond you, nor exult over what cometh to you; for God loveth not any presumptuous boasters,

Who are covetous and commend covetousness to men. But whoso turneth away,—verily God is Rich and worthy to be praised.

We sent Our Apostles with manifestations, and We sent down by them the Book and the Balance, that men might stand upright in equity, and We sent down IRON, wherein is great strength and uses for men,—and that God might know who would help Him and His Apostles in secret: verily God is strong and mighty.

And we sent Noah and Abraham, and we gave their seed prophecy in the Scripture: and some of them are guided, but many are disobedient.

Then we sent our apostles in their footsteps, and we sent Jesus the Son of Mary, and gave him the Gospel, and put in the hearts of those that follow him kindness and pitifulness;

but monkery, they invented it themselves! We prescribed it not to them—save only to seek the approval of God, but they did not observe this with due observance. Yet we gave their reward to those of them that believed, but many of them were transgressors.

O ye who believe, fear God and believe in His Apostle; He will give you a double portion of His mercy, and will set you a light to walk by, and will forgive you: for God is forgiving and merciful:—

That the People of the Scripture may know that they have not power over aught of God's grace; and that grace is in the hands of God alone, who giveth to whom He pleaseth: and God is the fount of boundless grace.

(lvii.)

THE VICTORY.

In the Name of God, the Compassionate, the Merciful.

VERILY we have won for thee a clear VICTORY—
That God may forgive thee thy former and latter sins, and fulfil His grace to thee, and guide thee on the straight way,
And that God may help thee mightily.
He it is who sent down peace into the hearts of the faithful, to strengthen their faith with faith, (for God's are the armies of the heavens and the earth, and God is All-knowing and Wise:)
To bring the faithful, men and women, into gardens beneath which rivers flow, to dwell therein for ever, and to take away their offences; and that is the great prize with God:
And to torment the hypocrites and the idolaters, men and women, who think of God an evil thought; there shall come upon them a turn of evil, and God is wroth with them and hath cursed them, and hath prepared Hell for them, and evil shall be their journey.

God's are the armies of the heavens and the earth, and God is Mighty and Wise!

Verily we have sent thee as a witness and a herald of gladness and a warner,
That ye may believe in God and in His Apostle; and may revere Him, and honour Him, and magnify Him morning and evening.
In truth, they who swear fealty to thee, do but swear fealty to God: the hand of God is upon their hands! Whosoever therefore breaketh it, breaketh it only to his own hurt; but whosoever is true to what he hath covenanted with God, He will give him a great reward.

The Arabs of the desert who were left behind will say to thee, "Our property and our families employed us; so ask pardon for us." They speak with their tongues what is not in their hearts. Say: But who can obtain aught for you from God, if He design for you harm, or design for you benefit? Nay, God is acquainted with what ye do!
Nay, ye thought that the Apostles and the faithful would not come back to their families any more, and that seemed good in your hearts,

and ye thought an evil thought, and ye are a lost people.

And whosoever believeth not in God and His Apostle . . . . . verily we have made ready a flame for the unbelievers!

And God's is the kingdom of the heavens and of the earth; He forgiveth whom He will, and He tormenteth whom He will: and God is Forgiving, Merciful!

They who were left behind will say when ye go forth to the spoil to take it, "Let us follow you." They would fain change the Word of God. Say: Ye shall by no means follow us; thus hath God said already. Then they will say, "Nay, ye are jealous of us." Nay, they are men of but little understanding.

Say to those who were left behind of the Arabs of the desert, Ye shall be called out against a people of mighty valour; ye shall fight with them, or they shall profess Islām. If, therefore, ye obey, God will bring you a goodly reward; but if ye turn your backs as ye turned your backs before, He will torment you with aching torment.

For the blind it is no crime, and for the lame no crime, and for the sick no crime [to turn the back.] And whoso obeyeth God and His

Apostle He shall bring him into gardens whereunder rivers flow: but whoso turneth his back, He will torment him with aching torment.

Well-pleased was God with the believers, when they sware fealty to thee under the tree; and He knew what was in their hearts: therefore did He send down tranquillity upon them, and rewarded them with a victory near at hand,

And many spoils to take, for God is Mighty and Wise!

God promised you many spoils to take, and sped this for you; (and He held back men's hands from you, that it might be a sign to the faithful, and that He might guide you on the straight way;)

And other spoils which ye could not take: but now hath God compassed it, for God is powerful over all.

If the unbelievers had fought against you, they would assuredly have turned their backs; then would they have met with no protector or helper.

This is God's way which prevailed before: and no changing wilt thou find in God's way.

And He it was who held back their hands from

you, and your hands from them, in the valley of Mekka, after that He had given you the victory over them; for God ever seeth what ye do.

These are they who believed not, and kept you away from the Sacred Mosque, as well as the offering, which was prevented from reaching its destination. And but for the faithful men and women, whom ye did not know and might have trampled, so that guilt might have lighted on you on their account without your knowledge, that God might bring whom He pleased into His mercy; had they been separate, we had surely punished the unbelievers among them with a grievous torment.

When the unbelievers had put disdain in their hearts,—the disdain of ignorance,—God sent down His tranquillity on His Apostle and the faithful, and fixed firmly in them the word of piety, for they were most worthy and fit for it, and God well knoweth all things.

Now hath God spoken truth to His Apostle in the night vision: "Ye shall surely enter the Sacred Mosque, if God please, safe, with shaven heads, or hair cut; ye shall not fear, for He knoweth what ye do not know; and

He hath ordained you, besides that, a victory near at hand."

It is He who hath sent his Apostle with the guidance and the religion of truth, to make it triumph over every religion; and God is witness enough!

Mohammad is the Apostle of God, and those of his party are vehement against the infidels, but compassionate to one another. Thou mayest see them bowing down, worshipping, seeking grace from God, and His approval; their tokens are on their faces—the traces of their prostrations. This is their likeness in the Torah, and their likeness in the Gospel, like a seed which putteth forth its stalk, and strengtheneth it, and it groweth stout, and standeth up upon its stem, rejoicing the sowers — to anger unbelievers thereby. To those among them who believe, and do the things that are right, God hath promised forgiveness and a mighty reward.

(xlviii.)

HELP.

In the Name of God, the Compassionate, the Merciful.

WHEN the HELP of God and victory come,
And thou seest the people entering the religion of God in troops;
Then magnify the praises of thy Lord, and seek forgiveness of Him; verily He is ever relenting.

(cx.)

THE LAW
GIVEN AT MEDINA

RELIGIOUS LAW.

It is not righteousness that ye turn your face towards the east or the west, but righteousness is [in] him who believeth in God and the Last Day, and the Angels, and the Scripture, and the Prophets, and who giveth wealth for the love of God to his kinsfolk and to orphans and the needy and the son of the road and them that ask and for the freeing of slaves, and who is instant in prayer, and giveth the alms; and those who fulfil their covenant when they covenant, and the patient in adversity and affliction and in time of violence, these are they who are true, and these are they who fear God.—ii. 172.

Say: We believe in God, and what hath been sent down to thee, and what was sent down to Abraham, and Ishmael, and Isaac, and Jacob, and the tribes, and what was given to Moses, and to Jesus, and the prophets from their Lord,—we make no distinction between any of them,—and to Him are we resigned: and whoso desireth other than Resignation [Islām] for a religion, it shall certainly not be accepted from him, and in the life to come he shall be among the losers. —iii. 78, 79.

Observe the prayers, and the middle prayer, and stand instant before God. And if ye fear, then afoot or mounted; but when ye are safe remember God, how he taught you what ye did not know.—ii. 239, 240.

When the call to prayer soundeth on the Day of Congregation (Friday), then hasten to remember God, and abandon business; that is better for you if ye only knew: and when prayer is done, disperse in the land and seek of the bounty of God.—lxii. 9, 10.

Turn thy face towards the Sacred Mosque; wherever ye be, turn your faces thitherwards.—ii. 139.

Give alms on the path of God, and let not your hands cast you into destruction; but do good, for God loveth those who do good; and accomplish the pilgrimage and the visit to God: but if ye be besieged, then [send] what is easiest as an offering.—ii. 191.

They will ask thee what it is they must give in alms. Say: Let what good ye give be for parents, and kinsfolk, and the orphan, and the needy, and the son of the road; and what good ye do, verily God knoweth it.—ii. 211.

They will ask thee what they shall expend in alms; say, The surplus.—ii. 216.

RELIGIOUS LAW. 135

If ye give alms openly, it is well; but if ye conceal it, and give it to the poor, it is better for you, and will take away from you some of your sins: and God knoweth what ye do.—ii. 273.

O ye who believe, make not your alms of no effect by taunts and vexation, like him who spendeth what he hath to be seen of men, and believeth not in God and the Last Day: for his likeness is as the likeness of a stone with earth upon it, and a heavy rain falleth upon it and leaveth it bare; they accomplish nothing with what they earn, for God guideth not the people that disbelieve. And the likeness of those who expend their wealth for the sake of pleasing God and for the certainty of their souls is as the likeness of a garden on a hill: a heavy rain falleth on it and it bringeth forth its fruit twofold; and if no heavy rain falleth on it, then the dew falleth; and God seeth what ye do. —ii. 266, 267.

Kind speech and forgiveness is better than alms which vexation followeth; and God is rich and ruthful.—ii. 265.

O ye who believe, there is prescribed for you the fast as it was prescribed for those before you; maybe ye will fear God for a certain number of days, but he amongst you who is sick or on a journey may fast a [like] number of other days. And for those who are able to fast [and do not], the expiation is feeding a poor man; but he who voluntarily doeth a good act, it is better for him; and to fast is better for you, if ye only knew. The month of Ramadān, wherein the Korān was sent down for guidance to men, and for proofs of the guidance, and the distinguishing [of good and evil]; whoso amongst you seeth this month, let him fast it; but he who is sick or on a journey, a [like] number of other days:—God wisheth for you what is easy, and wisheth not for you what is difficult—that ye may fulfil the number, and magnify God, in that He hath guided you;—and maybe ye will be thankful.—ii. 179-181.

Proclaim among the people a Pilgrimage: let them come to thee on foot and on every fleet camel, coming by every deep pass, to be present at its benefits to them, and to make mention of God's name at the appointed days over the beasts with which He hath provided them: then eat thereof, and feed the poor and needy; then let them end the neglect of their persons, and pay their vows, and make the circuit of the ancient House.—xxii. 28-30.

He only shall visit the Mosques of God who believeth in God and the Last Day, and is instant in prayer, and payeth the alms, and feareth God only.—ix. 18.

Do ye place the giving drink to the pilgrims, and the visiting of the Sacred Mosque, on the same level with him who believeth in God and the Last Day, and fighteth on the path of God? They are not equal in the sight of God.—ix. 19.

Fight in the path of God with those who fight with you;—but exceed not; verily God loveth not those who exceed.—And kill them wheresoever ye find them, and thrust them out from whence they thrust you out; for dissent is worse than slaughter; but fight them not at the Sacred Mosque, unless they fight you there: but if they fight you, then kill them: such is the reward of the infidels! But if they desist, then verily God is forgiving and merciful.—But fight them till there be no dissent, and the worship be only to God;—but, if they desist, then let there be no hostility save against the transgressors.—ii. 186-189.

They will ask thee of the sacred month, and fighting therein; say, Fighting therein is a great sin; but turning people away from God's path, and disbelief in Him and in the Sacred Mosque, and turning His people out therefrom, is a greater in God's sight, and dissent is a greater sin than slaughter.—ii. 214.

Forbidden to you is that which dieth of itself, and blood, and the flesh of swine, and that which is dedicated to other than God, and what is strangled, and what is killed by a blow, or by falling, and what is gored, and what wild beasts have preyed on—except what ye kill in time—and what is sacrificed to idols; and to divide by [the divination of] arrows, that is transgression in you.—v. 4.

Make not God the butt of your oaths, that ye will be pious and fear God, and make peace among men, for God heareth and knoweth.—ii. 224.

O ye who believe, verily wine and gambling and statues and divining arrows are only an abomination of the devil's making: avoid them then; haply ye may prosper.—v. 92.

CIVIL AND CRIMINAL LAW.

It is not for a believer to kill a believer, but by mistake; and whoso killeth a believer by mistake must free a believing slave; and the blood-wit must be paid to his family, unless they remit it in alms; but if he be of a people hostile to you, and yet a believer, then let him only free a believing slave, and if it be a tribe between whom and you there is an alliance, then let the blood-wit be paid to his family, and let him free a believing slave; but if he cannot find the means, then let him fast for two consecutive months—a penance from God: for God is all-knowing and wise. And whoso killeth a believer on purpose, his reward is Hell, to abide therein for ever, and God will be wroth with him, and curse him, and prepare for him a mighty torment.—iv. 94, 95.

O ye who believe! Retaliation is prescribed for you for the slain: the free for the free, the slave for the slave, the woman for the woman, yet for him who is remitted aught by his brother, shall be prosecution in reason, and payment in generosity.—ii. 173.

He who slayeth a soul, unless it be for another soul, or for wickedness in the land, is as though he had slain all mankind; and he who saveth a soul alive is as though he had saved the lives of all mankind.—v. 35.

The reward of those who war against God and His apostle, and work evil in the earth, is but that they shall be killed or crucified, or that their hands and feet shall be cut off alternately, or that they shall be banished from the land—that is their disgrace in this world, and in the next they shall have a mighty torment.—v. 37.

The man thief and the woman thief, cut off the hands of both in requital for what they have done; an example from God, for God is mighty and wise.—v. 42.

They who devour usury shall not rise again, save as he riseth whom the Devil hath smitten with his touch; that is because they say, " Selling is only like usury:" but God hath allowed selling, and forbidden usury.—ii. 276.

If ye fear that ye cannot do justice between orphans, then marry such women as are lawful to you, by twos or threes or fours; and if ye fear ye cannot be equitable, then only one, or what [slaves] your right hands possess: that is the chief thing—that ye be not unfair.—iv. 3.

Marry those of you who are single, and the good among your servants, and your handmaidens. If they be poor, God of his bounty will enrich them, and God is liberal, wise. And let those who cannot find a match, live in chastity, till God of His bounty shall enrich them.—xxiv. 32.

Wed not idolatrous women until they believe, for surely a believing handmaiden is better than an idolatress, although she captivate you. And wed not idolaters until they believe, for a believing slave is better than an idolater, although he charm you.—ii. 220.

Divorce may be twice : then take them in reason or let them go with kindness. It is not lawful for you to take from them aught of what ye have given them, unless both fear that they cannot keep God's bounds. But if he divorce her [a third time], she is not lawful to him afterwards, until she marry another husband; but if he also divorce her, it is no crime in them both to come together again.—ii. 229, 230.

And for the divorced there should be a maintenance in reason, a duty this on those who fear God.—ii. 242.

Against those of your women who commit adultery, summon witnesses four in number from among you ; and if these bear witness [to the crime], then keep the women in houses till death release them, or God make a way for them.—iv. 19.

They who slander chaste women, and bring not four witnesses, scourge them with fourscore stripes, and receive not their testimony for ever, for these are the transgressors:—save those who afterwards repent and do what is right—for God is forgiving, merciful.—xxiv. 4.

It is prescribed for you that, when one of you is at the point of death, if he leave property, the legacy is to his parents and to his kindred in reason—a duty upon those that fear God.—ii. 176.

God ordereth you concerning your children: for a male, the equal of the portion of two females, and if there be more than two women, let them have two-thirds of what [the deceased] hath left; and if there be only one, then let her have the half; and for the parents, for each of them a sixth of what he hath left, if he hath issue; but if he hath no issue, and his parents inherit, then let his mother have a third; and if he hath brethren, let his mother have a sixth, after payment of any bequest he may have bequeathed, or debts. Your parents and your children, ye know not which is the more helpful to you. An ordinance from God: verily God is all-knowing and wise! And yours is half of what your wives leave, if they have no issue; but if they have issue, then ye shall have a fourth of what they leave, after payment of any bequests they may bequeath, or their debts; and they shall have a fourth of what ye leave, if ye have no issue; but if ye have issue, then let them have an eighth of what ye leave, after paying of any bequest ye may bequeath, or debts. And if the man's or the woman's heir be a collateral kinsman, and he (or she) have a brother or a sister, then let each of these two have a sixth; but if they are more than that, let them share a third, after payment of any bequests he may bequeath, or debts, without prejudice; an ordinance from God, and God is wise and clement!

These are God's statutes, and whoso obeyeth God and the Apostle, He will bring him into gardens, whereunder rivers flow, to abide therein for aye, — that is the great prize! But whoso rebelleth against God and his Apostle, and transgresseth His statutes, He will bring him into fire, to dwell therein for aye; and his shall be a shameful torment.—iv. 12-18.

Those of you who die and leave wives, should leave their wives maintenance for a year, without driving them out [from their homes]: but if they go out, there is no crime in you for what they do for themselves in reason ; and God is mighty and wise.—ii. 241.

If a man perish and leave no issue, but leave a sister, then hers is half of what he leaves, and he shall be her heir, if she have no issue; but if there be two sisters, let them have two-thirds of what he leaves, and if there be brethren, both men and women, let the male have the equal of the portion of two females. God maketh this plain to you, lest ye err; and God knoweth all things.—iv. 176.

O ye who believe! stand fast by justice, bearing witness before God, though it be against yourselves, or your parents, or your kindred, whether it be rich or poor; for God is worthier than they.—iv. 134.

To those of your slaves who desire a deed [for buying their freedom], write it for them, if ye know good in them, and give them a portion of the wealth of God which He hath given you.—xxiv. 33.

If any of the idolaters seek refuge with thee, grant him refuge, that he may hear the word of God; then let him reach his place in safety.—ix. 6.

God wisheth to make it light for you, for man was created weak.—iv. 32.

If ye shun great sins which ye are forbidden, we will cover your offences, and make you enter Paradise with a noble entrance.—iv. 35.

THE

TABLE-TALK

OF

MOHAMMAD

L

THE TABLE-TALK OF MOHAMMAD.

WHEN God created the creation He wrote a book, which is near him upon the sovran Throne; and what is written in it is this: *Verily my compassion overcometh my wrath.*

Say not, if people do good to us, we will do good to them, and if people oppress us, we will oppress them: but resolve that if people do good to you, you will do good to them, and if they oppress you, oppress them not again.

God saith: Whoso doth one good act, for him are ten rewards, and I also give more to whomsoever I will; and whoso doth ill, its retaliation is equal to it, or else I forgive him; and he who seeketh to approach me one cubit, I will seek to approach him two fathoms; and he who walketh towards me, I will run towards him; and he who cometh before me with the earth full of sins, but joineth no Partner to me, I will come before him with an equal front of forgiveness.

There are seven people whom God will draw under His own shadow, on that Day when there will be no other shadow : one a just king ; another, who hath employed himself in devotion from his youth ; the third, who fixeth his heart on the Mosque till he return to it ; the fourth, two men whose friendship is to please God, whether together or separate ; the fifth, a man who remembereth God when he is alone, and weepeth ; the sixth, a man who is tempted by a rich and beautiful woman, and saith, Verily I fear God ! the seventh, a man who hath given alms and concealed it, so that his left hand knoweth not what his right hand doeth.

The most excellent of all actions is to befriend any one on God's account, and to be at enmity with whosoever is the enemy of God.

Verily ye are in an age in which if ye abandon one-tenth of what is ordered, ye will be ruined. After this a time will come when he who shall observe one-tenth of what is now ordered will be redeemed.

Concerning Prayer.

Angels come amongst you both night and day; then those of the night ascend to heaven, and God asketh them how they left His creatures: they say, We left them at prayer, and we found them at prayer.

The rewards for the prayers which are performed by people assembled together are double of those which are said at home.

Ye must not say your prayers at the rising or the setting of the sun: so when a limb of the sun appeareth, leave your prayers until her whole orb is up: and when the sun beginneth to set, quit your prayers until the whole orb hath disappeared; for, verily she riseth between the two horns of the Devil.

No neglect of duty is imputable during sleep; for neglect can only take place when one is awake: therefore, when any of you forget your prayers, say them when ye recollect.

When any one of you goeth to sleep, the Devil tieth three knots upon his neck; and saith over every knot, "The night is long, sleep." Therefore, if a servant awake and remember God, it openeth one knot, and if he perform the ablution, it openeth another; and if he say prayers it openeth the other; and he riseth in the morning in gladness and purity:—otherwise he riseth in a lethargic state.

When a Muslim performeth the ablution, it washeth from his face those faults which he may have cast his eyes upon; and when he washeth his hands, it removeth the faults they may have committed, and when he washeth his feet, it dispelleth the faults towards which they may have carried him: so that he will rise up in purity from the place of ablution.

Of Charity.

When God created the earth, it began to shake and tremble; then God created mountains, and put them upon the earth, and the land became firm and fixed; and the angels were astonished at the hardness of the hills, and said, "O God, is there anything of thy creation harder than hills?" and God said, "Yes, water is harder than the hills, because it breaketh them?" Then the angel said, "O Lord, is there anything of thy creation harder than water?" He said, "Yes, wind overcometh water: it doth agitate it and put it in motion." They said, "O our Lord! is there anything of thy creation harder than wind?" He said, "Yes, the children of Adam giving alms: those who give with their right hand, and conceal from their left, overcome all."

The liberal man is near the pleasure of God and is near Paradise, which he shall enter into, and is near the hearts of men as a friend, and he is distant from hell; but the niggard is far from God's pleasure and from paradise, and far from the hearts of men, and near the Fire; and verily a liberal ignorant man is more beloved by God than a niggardly worshipper.

A man's giving in alms one piece of silver in his lifetime is better for him than giving one hundred when about to die.

Think not that any good act is contemptible, though it be but your brother's coming to you with an open countenance and good humour.

There is alms for a man's every joint, every day in which the sun riseth; doing justice between two people is alms; and assisting a man upon his beast, and his baggage, is alms; and pure words, for which are rewards; and answering a questioner with mildness is alms, and every step which is made toward prayer is alms, and removing that which is an inconvenience to man, such as stones and thorns, is alms.

The people of the Prophet's house killed a goat, and the Prophet said, "What remaineth of it?" They said, "Nothing but the shoulder; for they have sent the whole to the poor and neighbours, except a shoulder which remaineth." The Prophet said, "Nay, it is the whole goat that remaineth except its shoulder: that remaineth which they have given away, the rewards of which will be eternal, and what remaineth in the house is fleeting."

Feed the hungry, visit the sick, and free the captive if he be unjustly bound.

Of Fasting.

A keeper of fasts, who doth not abandon lying and slandering, God careth not about his leaving off eating and drinking.

Keep fast and eat also, stay awake at night and sleep also, because verily there is a duty on you to your body, not to labour overmuch, so that ye may not get ill and destroy yourselves; and verily there is a duty on you to your eyes, ye must sometimes sleep and give them rest; and verily there is a duty on you to your wife, and to your visitors and guests that come to see you; ye must talk to them; and nobody hath kept fast who fasted always; the fast of three days in every month is equal to constant fasting: then keep three days' fast in every month.

Of Reading the Korān.

The state of a Muslim who readeth the Korān is like the orange fruit, whose smell and taste are pleasant; and that of a Muslim who doth not read the Korān, is like a date which hath no smell, but a sweet taste; and the condition of any hypocrite who doth not read the Korān is like the colocynth which hath no smell, but a bitter taste; and the hypocrite who readeth the Korān is like the sweet bazil, whose smell is sweet, but taste bitter.

Read the Korān constantly; I sware by Him in the hands of whose might is my life, verily the Korān runneth away faster than a camel which is not tied by the leg.

Of Labour and Profit.

Verily the best things which ye eat are those which ye earn yourselves or which your children earn.

Verily it is better for one of you to take a rope and bring a bundle of wood upon his back and sell it, in which case God guardeth his honour, than to beg of people, whether they give him or not; if they do not give him, his reputation suffereth and he returneth disappointed; and if they give him, it is worse than that, for it layeth him under obligations.

A man came to the Prophet, begging of him something, and the Prophet said, " Have you nothing at home?" He said, "Yes, there is a large carpet, with one part of which I cover myself, and spread the other, and there is a wooden cup in which I drink water." Then the Prophet said, " Bring me the carpet and the cup." And the man brought them, and the Prophet took them in his hand and said, " Who will buy them?" A man said, " I will take them at one silver piece." He said, "Who will give more?" This he repeated twice or thrice. Another man said, "I will take them for two pieces of silver." Then the Prophet gave the carpet and cup to that man, and took the two pieces of silver, and gave them to the helper, and said, "Buy food with one of these pieces, and give it to your family, that they may make it their sustenance for a few days; and buy a hatchet with the other piece and bring it to me." And the man brought it; and the Prophet put a handle to it with his own hands, and then said, "Go, cut wood, and sell it, and let me not see you for fifteen days." Then the man went cutting wood, and selling it; and he came to the Prophet, when verily he had got ten pieces of silver, and he bought a garment with part of it, and food with part. Then the Prophet said, "This cutting and selling of wood, and making your livelihood by it, is better for you than coming on the day of resurrection with black marks on your face."

Acts of begging are scratches and wounds by which a man woundeth his own face; then he who wisheth to guard his face from scratches and wounds must not beg, unless that a man asketh from his prince, or in an affair in which there is no remedy.

The Prophet hath cursed ten persons on

account of wine: one, the first extractor of the juice of the grape for others; the second for himself; the third the drinker of it; the fourth the bearer of it; the fifth the person to whom it is brought; the sixth the waiter; the seventh the seller of it; the eighth the eater of its price; the ninth the buyer of it; the tenth that person who hath purchased it for another.

Merchants shall be raised up liars on the Day of Resurrection, except he who abstaineth from that which is unlawful, and doth not swear falsely, but speaketh true in the price of his goods.

The taker of interest and the giver of it, and the writer of its papers and the witness to it, are equal in crime.

The holder of a monopoly is a sinner and offender.

The bringers of grain to the city to sell at a cheap rate gain immense advantage by it, and he who keepeth back grain in order to sell at a high rate is cursed.

He who desireth that God should redeem him

from the sorrows and difficulties of the Day of Resurrection, must delay in calling on poor debtors, or forgive the debt in part or whole.

A martyr shall be pardoned every fault but debt.

Whosoever has a thing with which to discharge a debt, and refuseth to do it, it is right to dishonour and punish him.

A bier was brought to the Prophet, to say prayers over it. He said, "Hath he left any debts?" They said, "Yes." He said, "Hath he left anything to discharge them?" They said, "No." The Prophet said, "Say ye prayers over him, I shall not."

Give the labourer his wage before his perspiration be dry.

Of Fighting for the Faith.

We came out with the Prophet, with a part of the army, and a man passed by a cavern in which was water and verdure, and he said in his heart, "I shall stay here, and retire from the world." Then he asked the Prophet's permission to live in the cavern; but he said, "Verily I have not been sent on the Jewish religion, nor the Christian, to quit the delights of society; but I have been sent on the religion inclining to truth, and that which is easy, wherein is no difficulty or austerity. I swear by God, in whose hand is my life, that marching about morning and evening to fight for religion is better than the world and everything that is in it: and verily the standing of one of you in the line of battle is better than supererogatory prayers performed in your house for sixty years.

When the Prophet sent an army out to fight, he would say, March in the name of God and by His aid and on the religion of the Messenger of God. Kill not the old man who cannot fight, nor young children nor women; and steal not the spoils of war, but put your spoils together; and quarrel not amongst yourselves, but be good to one another, for God loveth the doer of good.

Of Judgments.

The first judgment that God will pass on man at the Day of Resurrection will be for murder.

Whosoever throweth himself from the top of a mountain and killeth himself is in Hell Fire for ever; and whosoever killeth himself with iron, his iron shall be in his hand, and he will stab his belly with it in Hell Fire everlastingly.

No judge must decide between two persons whilst he is angry.

There is no judge who hath decided between men, whether just or unjust, but will come to God's court on the Day of Resurrection held by the neck by an angel; and the angel will raise his head towards the heavens and wait for God's orders; and if God ordereth to throw him into hell, the angel will do it from a height of forty years' journey.

Verily there will come on a just judge at the Day of Resurrection such fear and horror, that he will wish, Would to God that I had not decided between two persons in a trial for a single date.

Of Women and Slaves.

The world and all things in it are valuable, but the most valuable thing in the world is a virtuous woman.

I have not left any calamity more hurtful to man than woman.

A Muslim cannot obtain (after righteousness) anything better than a well-disposed, beautiful wife: such a wife as, when ordered by her husband to do anything, obeyeth; and if her husband look at her, is happy; and if her husband swear by her to do a thing, she doth it to make his oath true; and if he be absent from her, she wisheth him well in her own person by guarding herself from inchastity, and taketh care of his property.

Verily the best of women are those who are content with little.

Admonish your wives with kindness; for women were created out of a crooked rib of Adam, therefore if ye wish to straighten it, ye will break it; and if ye let it alone, it will be always crooked.

Every woman who dieth, and her husband is pleased with her, shall enter into paradise.

That which is lawful but disliked by God is divorce.

A woman may be married by four qualifications: one, on account of her money; another, on account of the nobility of her pedigree; another, on account of her beauty; a fourth, on account of her faith; therefore look out for religious women, but if ye do it from any other consideration, may your hands be rubbed in dirt.

A widow shall not be married until she be consulted; nor shall a virgin be married until her consent be asked, whose consent is by her silence.

When the Prophet was informed that the people of Persia had made the daughter of Chosroes their Queen, he said, The tribe that constitutes a woman its ruler will not find redemption.

Do not prevent your women from coming to the mosque; but their homes are better for them.

O assembly of women, give alms, although it be of your gold and silver ornaments; for verily ye are mostly of Hell on the Day of Resurrection.

When ye return from a journey and enter your town at night, go not to your houses, so that your wives may have time to comb their dishevelled hair.

God has ordained that your brothers should be your slaves: therefore him whom God hath ordained to be the slave of his brother, his brother must give him of the food which he eateth himself, and of the clothes wherewith he clotheth himself, and not order him to do anything beyond his power, and if he doth order such a work, he must himself assist him in doing it.

He who beateth his slave without fault, or slappeth him in the face, his atonement for this is freeing him.

A man who behaveth ill to his slave will not enter into paradise.

Forgive thy servant seventy times a day.

Of Dumb Animals.

Fear God in respect of animals: ride them when they are fit to be ridden, and get off when they are tired.

A man came before the Prophet with a carpet, and said, "O Prophet! I passed through a wood, and heard the voices of the young of birds; and I took and put them into my carpet; and their mother came fluttering round my head, and I uncovered the young, and the mother fell down upon them, then I wrapped them up in my carpet; and there are the young which I have." Then the Prophet said, "Put them down." And when he did so, their mother joined them: and the Prophet said, "Do you wonder at the affection of the mother towards her young? I swear by Him who hath sent me, verily God is more loving to His servants than the mother to these young birds. Return them to the place from which ye took them, and let their mother be with them."

Verily there are rewards for our doing good to dumb animals, and giving them water to drink. An adulteress was forgiven who passed by a dog at a well; for the dog was holding out his tongue from thirst, which was near killing him; and the woman took off her boot, and tied it to the end of her garment, and drew water for the dog, and gave him to drink; and she was forgiven for that act.

Of Hospitality.

When a man cometh into his house and remembereth God and repeateth His name at eating his meals, the Devil saith to his followers, " Here is no place for you to stay in to-night, nor is there any supper for you." And when a man cometh into his house without remembering God's name, the Devil saith to his followers, " You have got a place to spend the night in."

Whosoever believeth in God and the Day of Resurrection must respect his guest, and the time of being kind to him is one day and one night, and the period of entertaining him is three days, and after that, if he doth it longer, he benefiteth him more. It is not right for a guest to stay in the house of the host so long as to inconvenience him.

I heard this, that God is pure, and loveth purity; and God is liberal, and loveth liberality; God is munificent, and loveth munificence: then keep the courts of your house clean, and do not be like Jews who do not clean the courts of their houses.

Of Government.

Government is a trust from God, and verily government will be at the Day of Resurrection a cause of inquiry, unless he who hath taken it be worthy of it and have acted justly and done good.

Verily a king is God's shadow upon the earth; and every one oppressed turneth to him: then when the king doeth justice, for him are rewards and gratitude from his subject: but, if the king oppresseth, on him is his sin, and for the oppressed resignation.

That is the best of men who disliketh power. Beware! ye are all guardians; and ye will be asked about your subjects: then the leader is the guardian of the subject, and he will be asked respecting the subject; and a man is a shepherd to his own family, and will be asked how they behaved, and his conduct to them; and a wife is guardian to her husband's house and children, and will be interrogated about them; and a slave is a shepherd to his master's property, and will be asked about it, whether he took good care of it or not.

There is no prince who oppresseth the subject and dieth, but God forbiddeth Paradise to him.

If a negro slave is appointed to rule over you, hear him, and obey him, though his head should be like a dried grape.

There is no obedience due to sinful commands, nor to any other than what is lawful.

O Prophet of God, if we have princes over us, wanting our rights, and withholding our rights from us, then what do you order us? He said, "Ye must hear them and obey their orders: it is on them to be just and good, and on you to be obedient and submissive."

He is not strong or powerful who throws people down, but he is strong who withholds himself from anger.

When one of you getteth angry, he must sit down, and if his anger goeth away from sitting, so much the better; if not, let him lie down.

Of Vanities and Sundry Matters.

The angels are not with the company with which is a dog nor with the company with which is a bell.

A bell is the Devil's musical instrument.

The angels do not enter a house in which is a dog, nor that in which there are pictures.

Every painter is in Hell Fire; and God will appoint a person at the Day of Resurrection for every picture he shall have drawn, to punish him, and they will punish him in Hell. Then if you must make pictures, make them of trees and things without souls.

Whosoever shall tell a dream, not having dreamt, shall be put to the trouble at the Day of Resurrection of joining two barleycorns; and he can by no means do it; and he will be punished. And whosoever listeneth to others' conversation, who dislike to be heard by him, and avoid him, boiling lead will be poured into his ears at the Day of Resurrection. And whosoever draweth a picture shall be punished by ordering him to breathe a spirit into it, and this he can never do, and so he will be punished as long as God wills.

O servants of God use medicine: because God hath not created a pain without a remedy for it, to be the means of curing it, except age; for that is a pain without a remedy.

He who is not loving to God's creatures and to his own children, God will not be loving to him.

The truest words spoken by any poet are those of Lebīd, who said, "Know that everything is vanity except God."

Verily he who believeth fighteth with his sword and tongue: I swear by God, verily abuse of infidels in verse is worse to them than arrows.

Meekness and shame are two branches of faith, and vain talking and embellishing are two branches of hypocrisy.

The calamity of knowledge is forgetfulness, and to lose knowledge is this, to speak of it to the unworthy.

Whoso pursueth the road of knowledge, God will direct him to the road of Paradise; and verily the angels spread their arms to receive him who seeketh after knowledge; and everything in heaven and earth will ask grace for him; and verily the superiority of a learned man over a mere worshipper is like that of the full moon over all the stars.

Hearing is not like seeing: verily God acquainted Moses of his tribe's worshipping a calf, but he did not throw down the tables; but when Moses went to his tribe, and saw with his eyes the calf they had made, he threw down the tables and broke them.

Be not extravagant in praising me, as the Christians are in praising Jesus, Mary's Son, by calling him God, and the Son of God; I am only the Lord's servant; then call me the servant of God, and His messenger.

It was asked, "O Messenger of God, what relation is most worthy of doing good to?" He said, "Your mother," this he repeated thrice: "and after her your father, and after him your other relations by propinquity.'

God's pleasure is in a father's pleasure, and God's displeasure is a father's displeasure.

Verily one of you is a mirror to his brother: Then if he see a vice in his brother he must tell him to get rid of it.

The best person near God is the best amongst his friends; and the best of neighbours near God is the best person in his own neighbourhood.

Deliberation in undertaking is pleasing to God, and haste is pleasing to the devil.

The heart of the old is always young in two things, in love for the world and length of hope.

Of Death.

Wish not for death any one of you; either a doer of good works, for peradventure he may increase them by an increase of life; or an offender, for perhaps he may obtain the forgiveness of God by repentance.

When the soul is taken from the body, the eyes follow it, and look towards it: on this account the eyes remain open.

When a believer is nearly dead, angels of mercy come, clothed in white silk garments, and say to the soul of the dying man, " Come out, O thou who art satisfied with God, and with whom He is satisfied; come out to rest, which is with God, and the sustenance of God's mercy and compassion, and to the Lord, who is not angry." Then the soul cometh out like the smell of the best musk, so that verily it is handed from one angel to another, till they bring it to the doors of the celestial regions. Then the angels say, " What a wonderful pleasant smell this is which is come to you from the earth!" Then they bring it to the souls of the faithful, and they are very happy at its coming; more than ye are at the coming of one of your family after a long journey. And the souls of the faithful ask it, "What hath such an one done, and such an one? how are they?" and they mention the names of their friends who are left in the world. And some of them say, "Let it alone, do not ask it, because it was grieved in the world, and came from thence aggrieved; ask it when it is at rest." Then the soul saith when it is at ease, "Verily such an one about whom ye ask is dead." And as they do not see him amongst themselves, they say to one another, "Surely he was carried to his mother, which is Hell Fire."

And verily when an infidel is near death, angels of punishment come to him, clothed in sackcloth, and say to his soul, "Come out, thou discontented, and with whom God is displeased; come to God's punishments." Then it cometh out with a disagreeable smell, worse than the worst stench of a dead body, until they bring it upon the earth, and they say, "What an extraordinary bad smell this is;" till they bring it to the souls of the infidels.

A bier was passing, and the Prophet stood up for it; and we stood with him and said, O Prophet! verily this bier is of a Jewish woman; we must not respect it." Then the Prophet said, "Verily death is dreadful: therefore when ye see a bier stand up."

Do not abuse or speak ill of the dead, because they have arrived at what they sent before them; they have received the rewards of their actions; if the reward is good, you must not mention them as sinful; and if it is bad, perhaps they may be forgiven, but if not, your mentioning their badness is of no use.

Sit not upon graves, nor say your prayers fronting them.

Whoso consoleth one in misfortune, for him is a reward equal to that of the sufferer.

Whoso comforteth a woman who has lost her child will be covered with a garment in Paradise.

The Prophet passed by graves in Medina, and turned his face towards them, and said, "Peace be to you, O people of the graves. God forgive us and you! Ye have passed on before us, and we are following you."

Of the State after Death.

To whomsoever God giveth wealth, and he doth not perform the charity due from it, his wealth will be made into the shape of a serpent on the Day of Resurrection, which shall not have any hair upon its head, and this is a sign of its poison and long life, and it hath two black spots upon its eyes, and it will be twisted round his neck like a chain on the Day of Resurrection; then the serpent will seize the man's jaw-bones, and will say, " I am thy wealth, the charity for which thou didst not give, and I am thy treasure, from which thou didst not separate any alms."

The Prophet asked us, " Did any one of you dream?" We said, " No." He said, " But I did. Two men came to me and took hold of my hands, and carried me to a pure land: and behold, there was a man sitting and another standing: the first had an iron hook in his hand, and was hooking the other in the lip, and split it to the back of the neck, and then did the same with the other lip. While this was doing the first healed, and the man kept on from one lip to the other." I said, " What is this?" They said, " Move on," and we did so till we reached a man sleeping on his back, and another standing at his head with a stone in his hand, with which he was breaking the other's head, and afterwards rolled the stone about and then followed it, and had not yet returned, when the man's head was healed and well. Then he broke it again, and I said, "What is this?" They said, "Walk on," and we walked, till we came to a hole like an oven, with its top narrow and its bottom wide, and fire was burning under it, and there were naked men and women in it; and when the fire burnt high the people mounted also, and when the fire subsided they subsided also. Then I said "What is this?" They said, "Move on," and we went on till we came to a river of blood, with a man standing in the middle of it, and another man on the bank, with stones in his hands: and when the man in the river attempted to come out, the other threw stones in his face, and made him return. And I said, "What is this?" They said, "Advance," and we moved forward, till we arrived at a green garden, in which was a large tree, and an old man and children sitting on the roots of it, and near it was a man lighting a fire. Then I was carried upon the tree, and put into a house which was in the middle of it,—a better house I have never seen: and there were old men, young men, women, and children. After that they brought me out of the house and carried me to the top of the tree, and put me into a better house, where were old men and young men. And I said to my two conductors, "Verily ye have shown me a great many things to-night, then inform me of what I have seen." They said, "Yes: as to the man whom you saw with split lips, he was a liar, and will be treated in that way till the Day of Resurrection; and the person you saw getting his head broken is a man whom God taught the Korān, and he did not repeat it in the night, nor practice what is in it by day, and he will be treated as you saw till the Day of Resurrection; and the people you saw in the oven are adulterers; and those you saw in the river are receivers of usury; and the old man you saw under the tree is Abraham; and the children around them are the children of men: and the person who was lighting the fire was Mālik, the keeper of hell; and the first house you entered was for the common believers; and as to the second house, it is for the martyrs: and we who conducted you are one of us Gabriel, and the other Michael; then raise up your head;" and I did so, and saw above it as it were a cloud: and they said, "That is your dwelling." I said, "Call it here, that I may enter it;" and they said, "Verily your life remaineth, but when you have completed it, you will come into your house."

When God created Paradise, He said to Gabriel, "Go and look at it," then Gabriel went and looked at it and at the things which God had prepared for the people of it. After that Gabriel came and said, "O my Lord! I swear by thy glory no one will hear a description of Paradise but will be ambitious of entering it." After that God surrounded Paradise with distress and troubles, and said, "O Gabriel, go and look at Paradise." And he went and looked, and then returned and said, "O my Lord, I fear that verily no one will enter it." And when God created Hell Fire He said to Gabriel, "Go and take a look at it." And he went and looked at it, and returned and said, "O my Lord, I swear by thy glory that no one who shall hear a description of Hell Fire will wish to enter it." Then God surrounded it with sins, desires, and vices, after that said to Gabriel, "Go and look at Hell Fire," and he went and looked at it, and said, "O my Lord, I swear by thy glory I am afraid that every one will enter Hell, because sins are so sweet that there is none but will incline to them."

If ye knew what I know of the condition of the resurrection and futurity, verily ye would weep much and laugh little.

Then I said, "O messenger of God! shall we perish while the virtuous are amongst us?" He said, Yes, when the wickedness shall be excessive, verily there will be tribes of my sects that will consider the wearing of silks and drinking liquor lawful, and will listen to the lute: and there will be men with magnificent houses, and their milch animals will come to them in the evening, full of milk, and a man will come begging a little and they will say, Come to-morrow. Then God will quickly send a punishment upon them, and will change others into the shape of monkeys and swine, unto the Day of Resurrection.

Verily among the signs of the Resurrection will be the taking away of knowledge from amongst men; and their being in great ignorance and much wickedness and much drinking of liquor, and diminution of men, and there being many women; to such a degree that there will be fifty women to one man, and he will work for a livelihood for the women.

How can I be happy, when Isrāfīl hath put the trumpet to his mouth to blow it, leaning his ear towards the true God for orders, and hath already knit his brow, waiting in expectation of orders to blow it?

Of Destiny.

The hearts of men are at the disposal of God like unto one heart, and He turneth them about in any way that He pleaseth. O Director of hearts, turn our hearts to obey Thee.

The first thing which God created was a pen, and He said to it, "Write." It said, "What shall I write?" And God said, "Write down the quantity of every separate thing to be created." And it wrote all that was and all that will be to eternity.

There is not one among you whose sitting-place is not written by God whether in the fire or in Paradise. The Companions said, "O Prophet! since God hath appointed our place, may we confide in this and abandon our religious and moral duty?" He said, "No, because the happy will do good works, and those who are of the miserable will do bad works."

The Prophet of God said that Adam and Moses (in the world of spirits) maintained a debate before God, and Adam got the better of Moses; who said, "Thou art that Adam whom God created by the power of His hands, and breathed into thee from His own spirit, and made the angels bow before thee, and gave thee an habitation in His own Paradise: after that thou threwest man upon the earth, from the fault which thou committedst." Adam said, "Thou art that Moses whom God elected for His prophecy, and to converse with, and He gave to thee twelve tables, in which are explained everything, and God made thee His confidant, and the bearer of His secrets: then how long was the Bible written before I was created?" Moses said, "Forty years." Then Adam said, "Didst thou see in the Bible that Adam disobeyed God?" He said, "Yes." Adam said, "Dost thou then reproach me on a matter which God wrote in the Bible forty years before creating me?"

'Aïsha relates that the Prophet said to her, "Do you know, O 'Aïsha! the excellence of this night?" (the fifteenth of Ramadān.) I said, "What is it, O Prophet?" He said, "One thing in this night is, that all the children of Adam to be born in the year are written down; and also those who are to die in it, and all the actions of the children of Adam are carried up to heaven in this night; and their allowances are sent down." Then I said, "O Prophet, do none enter Paradise except by God's mercy?" He said, "No, none enter except by God's favour:" this he said thrice. I said, "You, also, O Prophet! will you not enter into Paradise, excepting by God's compassion?" Then the Prophet put his hand on his head, and said, "I shall not enter, except God cover me with His mercy:" this he said thrice.

———

A man asked the Prophet what was the mark whereby a man might know the reality of his faith. He said, "If thou derive pleasure from the good which thou hast done, and be grieved for the evil which thou hast committed, thou art a true believer." The man said, "What doth a fault really consist in?" He said, "When anything pricketh thy conscience forsake it."

I am no more than man: when I order you anything with respect to religion, receive it, and when I order you about the affairs of the world then I am nothing more than man.

NOTES.

THE MEKKA SPEECHES.

I.—The Poetic Period.

The rhyming prose in which the Korān is written may be seen to best advantage in this earliest phase of Mohammad's oratory, when the sentences are short and the rhythm more *chantant* than in the later speeches. "The Smiting" (p. 7), will serve as a specimen of the sound of the original Arabic, as far as it can be represented in Roman characters:—

Bismi-llahi-r-rahmāni-r-rahīm
El-kāri'atu mā-l-kāri'ah
Wa-mā adrāka mā-l-kāri'ah
Yawma yekūnu-n-nāsu ke-l-farāsi-l-mabthūth
Wa-tekūnu-l-jibālu ke-l-'ihni-l-manfūsh
Fe-amma men thekulet mawāzīnuhu fe-huwa fī 'īshetin rādiyeh
Wa-amma men khaffet mawāzīnuhu fe-ummuhu hāwiyeh
Wa-mā adrāka mā hiyeh
Nārun hāmiyeh

The effect of which may be thus roughly preserved in English:—

In the Name of God, the Compassionate, the Merciful.
The Smiting! What is the Smiting?
And what shall teach thee what is the Smiting?
The Day when men shall be like moths adrift,
And the hills shall be like wool-flocks rift:
Then as for him whose scales are heavy, his shall be a life of bliss:
And as for him whose scales are light, a place in the Pit is his:
And what shall teach thee what that place is—
A Fire that blazes!

P. 3. THE NIGHT.—The formula "*In the Name of God, the Compassionate, the Merciful,*" precedes all the chapters of the Korān but one. *We.*—God speaks in the plural in the Korān.

P. 5. THE COUNTRY.—*The two highways:* the *steep one* to heaven, and the smooth one to hell.

P. 6. *The people of the right hand*—those that receive the book of the record of their actions in their right hand—the blessed. Contrariwise—*the people of the left hand*—the damned.

P. 7. THE SMITING.—One of many similar names for the Day of Judgment. *The Bottomless Pit,* "El-Hāwiyeh," is the lowest stage of the Hell of the Korān.

P. 8. THE QUAKING.—*Burdens, i.e.* the dead. *Her tidings:* "The tidings of the earth are these—she will bear witness to the actions of every man and woman done upon her surface."—Tradition of Mohammad.

P. 9. THE RENDING ASUNDER. — *Reporters:* two angels who note respectively the good and the evil deeds and words of every man.

P. 13. THE BACKBITER.—This speech is said to have been levelled at a personal enemy.
Blasting Hell, "El-Hutameh," is the third stage of the Mohammadan Inferno.

P. 14. THE SPLENDOUR OF MORNING.—Evidently uttered in a time of despondency and with the intention of self-encouragement.

P. 15. THE MOST HIGH.—*The books of eld.* Mohammad asserted that his doctrine was a revival of the religion of Abraham and the patriarchs, as it was before the Jews corrupted it.

P. 17. THE WRAPPING.—A simile from the wrapping of a head in a turban.

Camels ten months gone with young were the Arabs' most valuable property.

The child that was buried alive. Infanticide of female children was among the crimes of the ancient Arab.

The Books—in which men's actions are recorded.

Stars that hide, i.e. that set; or, as others say, "that retrogress," *i.e.* the planets.

P. 18. *Mad.* The people commonly believed Mohammad to be possessed with a jinni (or genius).

Pelted devil. The evil jinn or devils are supposed to act the eavesdropper on the confines of heaven, and to be driven away by shooting stars.

A reminder, scil., of the true religion of Abraham and the prophets, which men had forgotten. Cf. LANE : *Selections from the Kur-ān*, lxxxi. 15, 47, 48 (2d ed., Trubner's Oriental Series).

P. 19. THE NEWS.—One of the many names which Mohammad employed to bring home to his people the reality and fearfulness of the Last Day.

Tent-pegs. Mountains were believed to keep the earth steady, as pegs do a tent.

P. 22. THE FACT.—One of the names of the Last Day : the event which must inevitably happen.

Abasing the sinners, and *exalting* the righteous.

Three kinds: the "outstrippers," the "people of the

right hand," and the "people of the left hand." In the original the same word means "right hand" and "happiness," or "good omen;" contrariwise, "left hand" and "misfortune." Cp. the use of *dexter* and *sinister*. An instance of Mohammad's practice of playing upon the different senses of a word.

The outstrippers, *i.e.* those who are the first to adopt the true religion—the prophets and apostles, who shall be rewarded by being allowed to stand nearest to God in the next world. The following fifteen lines describe their happy fate; after which, fourteen refer to the *people of the right hand*, or ordinary believers; and then seventeen lines to the *people of the left hand*, or damned.

P. 24. *Zakkūm:* A thorny tree with a bitter fruit, which grows up from the bottomless pit.

P. 26. *Preserved Book.*—Mohammad taught that every "revelation" in the Korān was but a transcript from the pages of a great book, known as the "*Mother of the Book*," "preserved" under the throne of God. The sentence, *Let none touch it but the purified*, is commonly inscribed upon the cover of the Korān.

Those brought nearest, *i.e.* the *outstrippers*, or prophets.

P. 27. THE MERCIFUL.—*Then which of the bounties*, etc. A refrain or burden of this kind is rare in the Korān, and is in no other instance so often repeated. The *twain* are mankind and the jinn (or genii). "Jinn," it may be remarked, is a plural, and the singular is "jinni" (a genius), for the masculine, and "jinnīyeh" for the feminine.

The two Easts. The rising-places of the sun in summer

and winter; *the two Wests*, the corresponding setting-places.

P. 28. *Two notables*, or "weighty ones," *i.e.* men and jinn.

P. 32. THE UNITY.—This profession of faith is held by Muslims to be equal in value to a third of the whole Korān.

P. 33. THE FĀTIHAH, or "Opening" chapter, so called because it is placed at the beginning of the authorised arrangement of the Korān. It is the *Paternoster* of Islām, and is repeated many times in the five daily prayers of the Muslims, and on every solemn occasion.

II.—THE RHETORICAL PERIOD.

P. 39. THE KINGDOM. *Say:* *i.e.* God bids Mohammad say. It must never be forgotten that Mohammad is only supposed to recite what God wrote in the Preserved Book (see note to p. 26) before the world began.

P. 41. THE MOON.—*Sign*, *i.e.* miracle, which Mohammad insistently declared his inability to work.
The Summoner: the archangel Isrāfīl.
Called it a lie, *i.e.* denied the doctrine of one God and of a Day of Judgment.

P. 42. *Ad:* an ancient Arab people, destroyed in prehistoric days. See LANE: *Selections from the Kur-ān*, 60-62.
Thamūd: another tribe, which experienced a similar fate. See LANE, *ibid*.

P. 45. K.—As to the meaning of this letter of the Arabic alphabet, which gives a title to this speech, in the words of the Muslim commentator, "God alone knoweth what He meaneth by it."

A warner from among themselves. The Mekkans were offended that an angel was not sent to them as an apostle, instead of a mere man.

Marvellous thing: the Resurrection.

P. 46. *The people of Tubba':* the Himyarites of Arabia Felix.

A driver and a witness.—Two angels, who are supposed to carry on the ensuing colloquy with God.

P. 48. *A tyrant.*—Mohammad was sent to warn, not to compel the obedience and faith of his people.

P. 49. Y. S.—See note to K above, and to p. 87 below.

P. 50. *Plain Exemplar:* the *Preserved Book*, mentioned above (note to p. 26).

P. 51. *Enter into Paradise:* the people had stoned him to death.

P. 52. *Her resting-place.*—The sun is feminine in Arabic, and the moon masculine.

P. 55. *Poetry.*—It was a common charge against Mohammad that he was a mad poet.

P. 57. THE CHILDREN OF ISRAEL, otherwise called THE NIGHT JOURNEY, from the reference in the first verse to a dream in which Mohammad saw himself carried from the Kaaba (the *Sacred Mosque*) at Mekka, to the

Temple (the *Furthest Mosque*) at Jerusalem; upon which Mohammadan theologians have raised a noble superstructure of fable. The first verse is probably later than the rest. The *two sins* and punishments of the Jews have also greatly exercised the commentators' minds. What they were Mohammad probably did not very precisely know himself.

P. 60. *The son of the road, i.e.* the traveller.

P. 61. *A just cause:* apostacy, adultery, or murder.

P. 62. *Daughters from among the angels.*—The Arabs worshipped the angels and jinn as daughters of God; and it is against this polytheism and blasphemous relationship that Mohammad protests, whilst he never denies but contrariwise admits the existence of such spirits. Further on (p. 64) he refers to these angels and other Arabian divinities, as beings who are not to be invoked, since they can have no influence for good or ill, and who themselves are in hope and fear of God's mercy and torment, like human beings. It should be noticed that hitherto Mohammad has directed his preaching against disbelief in the One God, but has not pointedly attacked the idolatry of the Mekkans. In Y. S., however, he begins to speak of *other gods* (p. 55), and in the Third or Argumentative Period, the angels and jinn which the Mekkans worshipped, and represented in the shape of idols, are frequently denounced, especially under the name of *Partners* (see pp. 76, 84, 90, 92, 93, 97, 98, 103, 106, etc.)

P. 65. *The accursed tree:* Zakkūm, see note to p. 24. The full Koranic history of Adam and Eve, and how Iblīs, the father of the devils, refused to do homage to the father of mankind, may be read in LANE's *Selections*, pp. 49-52.

P. 67. *Well-nigh tempted:* referring apparently to an inclination of Mohammad to temporize with idolatry on a special occasion.

P. 68. *The Spirit:* Gabriel, the teacher of Mohammad, and the bearer of revelations from God to His prophet.

P. 71. *Call upon God, or call upon the Merciful.* — Mohammad's use of two general names for God had apparently caused some confusion among the faithful, which this verse removed.

The "Children of Israel" speech is especially important, since it contains more definite regulations of conduct than any other of the orations delivered at Mekka.

III.—THE ARGUMENTATIVE PERIOD.

P. 76. THE BELIEVER. *Twice hast thou given us death,* etc.—Referring to the absence of life before birth, and the deprivation of it at death, and to the being quickened at birth, and raised again after death.

P. 78. *Their footprints,* or vestiges : *i.e.* their buildings and public works.

Moses. For the Koranic history of the Israelites, see LANE's *Selections,* pp. 97-131.

P. 84. *I am bidden to resign myself:* i.e. I am bidden to become a Muslim, for *Muslim* (Moslem or Musulman) means "one who is resigned," and *Islām,* belonging to the same root, signifies "resignation," or "self-surrender." This is the correct name of the religion taught by the Arabian prophet, who would have regarded the epithet

"Mohammadan," as applied to the creed, or the professor thereof, as nothing short of blasphemy.

JONAH. P. 87. A. L. R.—Letters the import of which is as mysterious as K. and Y. S. before, and A. L. M. R. afterwards. Nöldeke believes them to be abbreviations of the names of the first reporters of the speeches.

P. 89. *I had dwelt a lifetime: i.e.* I should not have waited till I was forty before I began preaching, if I was the designing impostor you take me for.

P. 90. *Ye are in ships—and they run with them.*—The reader must have observed that sudden transitions from the second to the third person, and from the singular to the plural, are very common in the Korān. They may perhaps be regarded as convincing evidence of the fidelity of Mohammad's reporters.

P. 97. *God hath taken Him a son:* referring to the Christian doctrine.

P. 100. *Kibla:* The point towards which prayer must be said. See p. 134.

P. 101. *Now!*—The angel Gabriel is credited with this taunt.

THUNDER. P. 104. A. L. M. R.—Mystic letters as above; perhaps for AL-MogheyReh, as the first reporter of this particular speech.

P. 106. *Patrons, i.e.* Idols.

P. 108. *Join what God hath bidden to be joined: i.e.* believe in the whole series of prophets, and join good works to faith.

P. 111. *Mother of the Book.*—The Preserved Book mentioned before in THE FACT (see note to p. 26).

THE MEDINA SPEECHES.

DECEPTION. P. 117. *Obey God, and obey the Apostle.*—This is a sure indication of the Medina origin of at least this verse, for the self-importance of the phrase would have been inappropriate in Mohammad's weak and insignificant position at Mekka. (The speech is, however, by some ascribed to the Mekka division.) Further on the words *Believe in God and His Apostle* (in IRON, p. 118), and *They who swear fealty to thee do but swear fealty to God* (in VICTORY, p. 125), indicate the same spirit of self-exaltation which began with the prophet's prosperity at Medina.

IRON. P. 119. *Manifest signs:* the revelations contained in the Korān.

P. 122. *It is written in the Book: i.e.* Every event is set down in the Preserved Book before the event itself is created.

God is rich: i.e. He has no need of your grudging alms.

VICTORY. P. 124.—The victory in question was probably the peaceful but real triumph of the Truce of Hudeybia, in A.H. 6; though some commentators prefer to regard the speech as prophetical of the conquest of Mekka two years later.

P. 125. *The Arabs of the desert who were left behind* were certain tribes who held aloof from the pilgrimage towards Mekka, which ended in the Truce of Hudeybia. Mohammad punished them by refusing to allow them to share in the booty which soon after fell to the faithful in the Khaibar expedition; hence the reference on p. 126.

P. 128. *In the valley of Mekka:* referring to the Truce of Hudeybia. *Kept you away from the Sacred Mosque:* the Koreysh refused to allow Mohammad and his followers to enter Mekka or perform the pilgrimage; whereupon the truce was concluded, by which the pilgrimage was to take place (*Ye shall surely enter the Sacred Mosque*) in the following year (see Introduction, p. xlv.)

P. 129. *Traces: i.e.* dust from touching the ground.

P. 130. HELP.—Revealed after the conquest of Mekka, and shortly before Mohammad's death, and believed to have given him warning of it.

THE LAW GIVEN AT MEDINA.

The forty paragraphs arranged on pp. 133-144, contain, it is believed, all the definite ordinances of Mohammad as set forth in the Medina speeches, with the exception of some regulations relating to women. The bulk of the Medina speeches are indeed rather collections of separate decisions or "rulings" put together for convenience of reference by the Muslims themselves than separate and complete orations. But as the practical teaching is interspersed with frequent and verbose prophetical legends of the kind with which the reader is already perhaps only too familiar and with animadversions on the political parties of Medina, and similar ephemeral matters, it has been thought best to extract the marrow of these lengthy and composite harangues, and place them in some sort of connected order. Chapter II., for instance, "The Cow," contains 286 verses; the first half is filled with the usual arguments and illustrations, and the old stories about Adam and Moses; whilst the second half contains a certain number of laws and precepts mixed with many repetitions of the proofs and appeals to reason which occur in most of the preceding speeches: altogether, 29 verses out of 286 are needed for the purpose of showing what Mohammad actually prescribed in civil and religious law. For an account of the modern interpretation of this law, see LANE's *Modern Egyptians*, 5th ed. Ch. III.; SELL's *Faith of Islam;* and HUGHES' *Notes on Mohammadanism*, 2d ed. 1877.

P. 134. *Observe the prayer, and the middle prayer.* It is not easy to make out the five daily prayers of Islām in the Korān. In the speech entitled "Hūd" (Mekka, Third Period, xi. 116) it is enjoined: "Observe prayer at two ends of the day, and at two parts of the night"; and again, in "T. H." (xx. 130), the praises of God are to be celebrated "before the rising of the sun and before its setting, and at times of the night and at the ends of the day"; and in "The Greeks" (xxx. 17) praise is ordained "in the evening and in the morning, and at the evening and at noon." The Muslim commentators differ as to the application of these injunctions to the five times of prayer recognized throughout the Mohammadan world; which are (1) just after sunset, (2) at nightfall, (3) at daybreak, (4) just after noon, and (5) in the middle of the afternoon.

NOTES. 195

Turn thy face towards the Sacred Mosque: i.e. towards the Kaaba of Mekka. Originally Mohammad placed the Kibla, or direction of prayer, at Jerusalem; but after his disagreement with the Jews of Medina he reverted to the old Mekkan temple as the focus of Islām.

P. 135. It is enacted (ii. 183) that the fast is to be observed from the time when you can distinguish a white thread from a black thread in the morning, till night; but from nightfall till dawn the Muslim may eat and drink and enjoy himself.

P. 136. *Make mention of God's name over the beasts:* i.e. Sacrifice them, saying, "In the name of God."

P. 140. The Korān contains a list of prohibited degrees ("Women," iv. 26, 27), which comprises mothers and stepmothers, daughters, sisters, aunts, nieces, fostermothers, fostersisters, mothers-in-law, stepdaughters, daughters-in-law, and two sisters, and other men's wives.

P. 142. *Keep the women in houses.* Immuring was afterwards changed to stoning both the man and the woman.

TABLE-TALK OF MOHAMMAD.

P. 147. *Retaliation is equal.*—It is worth noticing, that while sin is requited with equal punishment or with forgiveness, good deeds are rewarded tenfold.

P. 150. *Rising or setting of the sun.*—The exact moment was forbidden, for fear of even the suspicion of sun-worship.

P. 164. It is recorded of the prophet, that when, being on a journey, he alighted at any place, he did not say his prayers until he had unsaddled his camel.

Chapters of the Korān translated in this Volume.

i. The Fatihah, p. 33.
x. Jonah, 87.
xiii. The Thunder, 104.
xvii. The Children of Israel, 57.
xxxvi. Y. S., 49.
xl. The Believer, 75.
xlviii. The Victory, 124.
l. K., 45.
liv. The Moon, 41.
lv. The Merciful, 27.
lvi. The Fact, 22.
lvii. Iron, 118.
lxiv. Deception, 115.
lxvii. The Kingdom, 37.
lxxviii. The News, 19.
lxxxi. The Wrapping, 17.
lxxxii. The Rending Asunder, 9.
lxxxvii. The Most High, 15.
xc. The Country, 5.
xcii. The Night, 3.
xciii. The Splendour of Morning, 14.
xcix. The Quaking, 8.
c. The Chargers, 11.
ci. The Smiting, 7.
civ. The Backbiter, 13.
cvii. Support, 12.
cx. Help, 130.
cxii. The Unity, 32.

Portions of Chapters, pp. 133-144.

ii. The Cow, 133-144.
iii. The Family of Imrān, 133.
iv. Women, 139, 140, 142-144.
v. The Table, 138, 140.
ix. Immunity, 136, 144.
xxii. The Pilgrimage, 136.
xxiv. The Light, 140, 141, 144.
lxii. The Congregation, 134.

THE END.

Printed by R. & R. Clark, *Edinburgh.*

THE GOLDEN TREASURY SERIES.

UNIFORMLY printed in 18mo, with Vignette Titles by J. E. MILLAIS, T. WOOLNER, W. HOLMAN HUNT, SIR NOEL PATON, ARTHUR HUGHES, &c. Engraved on Steel by JEENS. Bound in extra cloth, 4s. 6d. each volume. Also kept in morocco and calf bindings.

> "Messrs. Macmillan have, in their Golden Treasury Series, especially provided editions of standard works, volumes of selected poetry, and original compositions, which entitle this series to be called classical. Nothing can be better than the literary execution, nothing more elegant than the material workmanship."—BRITISH QUARTERLY REVIEW.

THE GOLDEN TREASURY OF THE BEST SONGS AND LYRICAL POEMS IN THE ENGLISH LANGUAGE. Selected and arranged, with Notes, by FRANCIS TURNER PALGRAVE.

THE CHILDREN'S GARLAND FROM THE BEST POETS. Selected and arranged by COVENTRY PATMORE.

THE BOOK OF PRAISE. From the best English Hymn Writers. Selected and arranged by LORD SELBORNE. *A New and Enlarged Edition.*

THE FAIRY BOOK; the Best Popular Fairy Stories. Selected and rendered anew by the Author of "JOHN HALIFAX, GENTLEMAN."

> "A delightful selection, in a delightful external form; full of the physical splendour and vast opulence of proper fairy tales."—SPECTATOR.

THE BALLAD BOOK. A Selection of the Choicest British Ballads. Edited by WILLIAM ALLINGHAM.

THE JEST BOOK. The Choicest Anecdotes and Sayings. Selected and arranged by MARK LEMON.

> "The fullest and best jest book that has yet appeared."—SATURDAY REVIEW.

BACON'S ESSAYS AND COLOURS OF GOOD AND EVIL. With Notes and Glossarial Index by W. ALDIS WRIGHT, M.A.

"The beautiful little edition of Bacon's Essays, now before us, does credit to the taste and scholarship of Mr. Aldis Wright."—SPECTATOR.

THE PILGRIM'S PROGRESS from this World to that which is to come. By JOHN BUNYAN.

"A beautiful and scholarly reprint."—SPECTATOR.

THE SUNDAY BOOK OF POETRY FOR THE YOUNG. Selected and arranged by C. F. ALEXANDER.

"A well-selected volume of sacred poetry."—SPECTATOR.

A BOOK OF GOLDEN DEEDS of All Times and All Countries. Gathered and Narrated Anew by the Author of "THE HEIR OF REDCLYFFE."

". . . To the young, for whom it is especially intended, as a most interesting collection of thrilling tales well told; and to their elders as a useful handbook of reference, and a pleasant one to take up when their wish is to while away a weary half-hour. We have seen no prettier giftbook for a long time."—ATHENÆUM.

THE ADVENTURES OF ROBINSON CRUSOE. Edited, from the Original Edition, by J. W. CLARK, M.A., Fellow of Trinity College, Cambridge.

THE REPUBLIC OF PLATO, TRANSLATED into ENGLISH, with Notes by J. LL. DAVIES, M.A., and D. J. VAUGHAN, M.A.

"A dainty and cheap little edition."—EXAMINER.

THE SONG BOOK. Words and Tunes from the best Poets and Musicians. Selected and arranged by JOHN HULLAH, Professor of Vocal Music in King's College, London.

"A choice collection of the sterling songs of England, Scotland, and Ireland, with the music of each prefixed to the words. How much true wholesome pleasure such a book can diffuse, and will diffuse, we trust, through many thousand families."—EXAMINER.

LA LYRE FRANCAISE. Selected and arranged, with Notes, by GUSTAVE MASSON, French Master in Harrow School.

"We doubt whether even in France itself so interesting and complete a repertory of the best French Lyrics could be found."—NOTES AND QUERIES.

TOM BROWN'S SCHOOL DAYS. By AN OLD BOY.

"A perfect gem of a book. The best and most healthy book about boys for boys that ever was written."—ILLUSTRATED TIMES.

A BOOK OF WORTHIES. Gathered from the Old Histories and written anew by the Author of "THE HEIR OF REDCLYFFE."

"An admirable addition to an admirable series."—WESTMINSTER REVIEW.

A BOOK OF GOLDEN THOUGHTS. By HENRY ATTWELL, Knight of the Order of the Oak Crown.

"Mr. Attwell has produced a work of rare value. . . . Happily it is small enough to be carried about in the pocket, and of such a companion it would be difficult to weary."—PALL MALL GAZETTE.

GUESSES AT TRUTH. By Two BROTHERS. *New Edition.*

THE CAVALIER AND HIS LADY. Selections from the Works of the First Duke and Duchess of Newcastle. With an Introductory Essay by EDWARD JENKINS, M.P., Author of "Ginx's Baby," &c.

"A charming little volume."—STANDARD.

THEOLOGIA GERMANICA. Edited by Dr. PFEIFFER, from the only complete Manuscript yet known. Translated from the German by SUSANNA WINKWORTH. With a Preface by the Rev. Charles Kingsley, and a Letter to the Translator by the Chevalier Bunsen, D.D.

SCOTCH SONG. A Selection of the Choicest Lyrics of Scotland. Compiled and arranged, with brief Notes, by MARY CARLYLE AITKIN.

"The book is one that should find a place in every library, we had almost said in every pocket."—SPECTATOR.

DEUTSCHE LYRIK: The Golden Treasury of the Best German Lyrical Poems. Selected and arranged, with Notes and Literary Introduction, by Dr. BUCHHEIM.

"A book which all lovers of German poetry will welcome."—WESTMINSTER REVIEW.

HERRICK: Selections from the Lyrical Poems. Arranged, with Notes, by F. T. PALGRAVE.

"For the first time the sweetest of English pastoral poets is placed within the range of the great world of readers."—ACADEMY.

POEMS OF PLACES. Edited by H. W. LONGFELLOW. England and Wales. Two Vols.

"A very happy idea, thoroughly worked out by an editor who possesses every qualification for the task."—SPECTATOR.

MATTHEW ARNOLD'S SELECTED POEMS

(Also a Large Paper Edition, Crown 8vo, 12s. 6d.)

"A volume which is a thing of beauty in itself."—PALL MALL GAZETTE.

THE STORY OF THE CHRISTIANS AND MOORS IN SPAIN. By C. M. YONGE, Author of "The Heir of Redclyffe." With Vignette by HOLMAN HUNT.

"This volume will prove a very attractive one."—JOHN BULL.

LAMB'S TALES FROM SHAKESPEARE. Edited by the Rev. A. AINGER, M.A., Reader at the Temple.

"Mr. Ainger's introduction is excellent."—SPECTATOR.

POEMS OF WORDSWORTH. Chosen and edited, with Preface, by MATTHEW ARNOLD. (Also a Large Paper Edition, Crown 8vo, 9s.)

"The selection is almost faultless."—SATURDAY REVIEW.

SHAKESPEARE'S SONNETS. Edited by F. T. PALGRAVE.

POEMS FROM SHELLEY. Selected and arranged by STOPFORD A. BROOKE, M.A. (Also a Large Paper Edition, Crown 8vo, 12s. 6d.)

"Full of power and true appreciation of Shelley's poetry."—SPECTATOR.

ESSAYS OF JOSEPH ADDISON. Chosen and edited by JOHN RICHARD GREEN, M.A., LL.D.

"This is a most welcome addition to a most excellent series."—EXAMINER.

SELECTIONS FROM BYRON. Chosen and arranged by MATTHEW ARNOLD. (Also a Large Paper Edition, Crown 8vo, 9s.)

"It is written in Mr. Arnold's neatest vein and in Mr. Arnold's most pellucid manner."—ATHENÆUM.

SIR THOMAS BROWNE'S RELIGIO MEDICI; Letter to a Friend, &c., and Christian Morals. Edited by W. A. GREENHILL, M.D., Oxon.

"Dr. Greenhill's annotations display care and research to a degree rare among English editors."—ATHENÆUM.

MACMILLAN & CO., LONDON.

www.ingramcontent.com/pod-product-compliance
Lightning Source LLC
Chambersburg PA
CBHW032138230426
43672CB00011B/2379